DOWN EAST MAINE

A World Apart

Dedicated to the memory of two inspired chroniclers of Maine:

Kosti Ruohomaa

and

E. B. White

each, in his way, a master of the telling observation.

Copyright © 1998 Frank Van Riper

ISBN 0-89272-448-X

2   3   4   5

Designed by Pat Marshall Design, Inc.

Printed by Oceanic Graphic Printing, Inc., Hong Kong

Down East Books

P.O. Box 679, Camden, Maine 04843

book orders: 1-800-766-1670

Library of Congress Cataloging-in-Publication Data

Van Riper, Frank.
    Down East Maine : a world apart / by Frank Van Riper.
        p.   cm.
    ISBN 0-89272-448-X (hardcover)
    1. Washington County (Me.)—Social life and customs. 2. Lubec
Region (Me.)—Social life and customs. 3. Washington County (Me.)—
Pictorial works. 4. Lubec Region (Me.)—Pictorial works.
5. Washington County (Me.)—Biography. 6. Lubec Region (Me.)—
Biography. 7. Van Riper, Frank. I. Title.
F27.W3V36   1998
974.1'42—dc21   98-34954
                                                        CIP

DOWN EAST MAINE

A World Apart

PHOTOGRAPHS AND TEXT BY FRANK VAN RIPER

DOWN EAST MAINE

A World Apart

*". . . Finally you run out of bridges, and you know
you made it."*

—Stephen King

It is a place of raw and fragile beauty where only the foolhardy challenge the tides, the winds, or the weather. Cities like Portland and Augusta may show the modern hand of progress; towns like Camden, Freeport, and Kennebunkport may bow under the suffocating weight of tourism. But much of Maine—especially the Maine depicted in this book—is untouched by the bustle and noise of the lower states. "The Way Life Should Be," it used to say in the ads.

In 1949, native son Kenneth Roberts wrote, "the southern portion of Maine—with its billboards, overnight camps, hot-dog stands and fried clam emporia—looks less like Maine than it does Massachusetts. It's axiomatic among those who have traveled widely in the state that you're not really in Maine and don't know what it ought to look like until you've crossed the Kennebec."

Roberts, whose description of the southern counties rings even truer today than it did nearly fifty years ago, clearly felt that the real Maine lay "down east," in the eastern coastal portion, which still resists change like a crotchety

uncle. To be sure, there are loomings: a few years ago, the easternmost McDonald's in the United States opened with great fanfare in Machias, featuring among the Big Macs and pseudo shakes something called a McLobster sandwich. But for every fast-food place there are scores more family-run diners featuring achingly fresh fish and homemade pie; for every big IGA supermarket, there are dozens of tiny groceries and general stores that will tend to you personally and run you a tab.

Though parts of the region—Blue Hill and Bar Harbor, for instance—can be bustling and tourist-dominated, down east Maine is still a place where you can walk in the woods for hours without encountering a soul; where the music of evening is in the birds and the crickets; and where the star-lit night sky—undimmed by competition from civilization below—burns with a rare, spectacular brilliance.

For at least two months every year, my wife Judy and I live in Lubec, the easternmost town in Maine's eastern-most county. It is from this base that we have come to love the land and people down east, and from which I began a five-year project of documentary photography and portraiture. To call Lubec poor is to understate the obvious. A few years ago, one of the town's major employers, McCurdy's Smokehouse, was shut down by the federal government for alleged health violations, even though this nation's last operating herring smokehouse had been going about its business without incident or complaint for generations. At this writing, it is problematic whether Lubec can afford to run its consolidated high school. Along the main street of the town, McCurdy's rugged, red-painted buildings sit boarded and empty next to the shells of other failed businesses. These days, Lubec resembles more a western ghost town than the quaint New England villages of poetry and postcard.

As is common in this part of Maine, many Lubeckers live in trailers, on property handed down for generations. It is land that, more often than not, affords spectacular views of places like Johnson Bay or Morrison Cove or Denbow Neck or Baileys Mistake. (Here and in other parts of down east Maine, you can often tell whether a person is a native by the placement of his or her dwelling. An out-sider will opt for the water view and, if brazen, will clear-cut the trees that block it. A Mainer, knowing that winter can be unforgiving—and taking the view for granted—will place home and truck near the road.) Yet the inexorable rise in property taxes—caused, in part, by escalating water-front land values—is forcing many of these same natives either to surrender their land to the town, or worse, to consider selling their birthright to people *from away*: wealthier outsiders who see in Lubec and the other parts of Washington County and adjoining Hancock County the last vestiges of America's coastal frontier.

What attracts such people—myself among them— is more than unspoiled beauty and tranquillity. It is the down-easters themselves who make this region so special, and that is the paradox: if ever they are forced to leave (for who knows where), something exceptional and vital will have been sapped from the land.

Hoping that this wouldn't happen, yet fearful that it might, I began to photograph people and places. With rare exceptions like Stephen King and Edmund Muskie, those depicted here are not famous and never will be. They are ordinary people making their way in an extraordinary place, and I photographed everywhere: from a crowded and frenzied tent-revival meeting to a tiny lobsterboat pitching in a cold November sea. I photographed in barns and in kitchens, in fish houses and in factories. I worked in shorts and in snowshoes. And everyplace I went, my camera was greeted first with curiosity and then with acceptance.

I grew up in New York City and have lived most of my life in Washington, D.C., save for one sabbatical year in Cambridge, Massachusetts, near Boston. My entire life has been spent in the three major urban centers of the Northeast. I always will be a city person. But rarely have I felt more comfortable or welcome than I do in down east Maine.

"The expression 'down east' came from the early days of coastal sailing," notes photographer/sailor Christopher Little. "Thundering up the coast, driven by the prevailing westerlies, propelled by acres of canvas, those exquisite clippers of commerce were sailing 'downwind toward the east'. . . or down east."

Author Stephen King defines down east in a way that conjures up the mythical Brigadoon. "I've lived in Maine my whole life," he told me after I shot his portrait, "and to me 'down east' is always one bridge farther east of where I am. . . . Finally, you run out of bridges, and you know you made it. As long as there's a bridge, you ain't down east."

By contrast, the farther one gets from Maine, the more inclusive the term becomes, so from far enough away the entire state is "down east." So romantic—and

tourist-attracting—has the term become that some visitors' maps try to claim the down east mantle for more commercially developed areas to the south. Ask a native, however, and you'll be told that down east Maine only begins east of the Penobscot River, hugging the rocky, rugged coast up to Passamaquoddy Bay and Grand Manan Channel, gateway to the Bay of Fundy.

Traveling down east requires effort—which is fine with most who live here. You can't do it by train—passenger service ended throughout the state in the mid-sixties, and talk about reviving some form of passenger-train service in the state has been limited to the Portland–Boston corridor. Though passenger steamships plied Maine's coastal waters in the last century, they are but a dim memory today. The

closest one can come by commercial jet is Bangor, still hours away by car from the farthest (and most beautiful) down east points. In Lubec, for example, the "airport" consists of a grassy field, Quonset hut, and windsock next to the town's one motel. (To find out if the Lubec field is cloaked in fog—a regular occurrence—pilots of small private planes often radio Bar Harbor, more than sixty miles down the coast. There, someone will telephone the motel in Lubec, and only after someone else looks out the window and relays the information to the Bar Harbor tower will a pilot know whether Lubec is actually clear for landing.)

My own first voyages to the area were less dramatic. I began exploring by car, driving up Route One—the

principal artery of coastal Maine—while attending the Maine Photographic Workshops in Rockport, some dozen years ago. There, my wife and I studied our craft, fell in love with the scenery and weather, and began looking for what we could afford to buy. Finding nothing in or near this wealthy mid-coast enclave, and not really wanting to be part of the ever-more-crowded and tourist-driven communities of Camden and Bar Harbor, we looked farther up the coast, farther east, until we finally ran out of bridges.

"It's called Washington County," a real-estate broker in Camden told us. "A lot of people down here think it's a joke. It's poor, and there's not much in the way of services. All I can tell you is that it's beautiful."

We looked at four properties, including one hard by the dump, and fell in love with a seven-acre parcel off Straight Bay Road on Morrison Cove. Typically, it had long ago been sold off by a local family to a previous summer resident. If we ever had any doubts about this being our place, they vanished when our golden retriever bounded from the car and into the icy-cold water barely a hundred yards from where we stood, surrounded by lush woods of pine and birch.

The clearing that day held only one building, a tumbling down one-room cabin, or camp. Its recent residents were porcupines, their leavings a pungent reminder. All Judy and I saw in the dark and gloomy place was an eyesore, and we made plans to tear it down. However, a few days later, reflecting the speed with which news can travel in a small community, our neighbor wandered by and changed our minds.

"I hear you're gonna tear down the camp," Art said to me. "I'll do it for nuthin' if I can keep the lumbah." The implication was clear: if we were going to demolish a perfectly serviceable building, at least we should not have to pay someone for our foolishness—nor waste good wood. We looked at the camp with new eyes. Later, our builder, Matt, remarked that, dismal though the camp looked, it had a straight roofline and a solid frame.

Over the next winter, he transformed it, putting in large windows facing the trees and the water. He added a bathroom, a new roof, and new cedar shingles but kept the unfinished interior and pine floor. It became for Judy and me our first Maine home and, later, the studio from which I now write. It never would have happened if Art hadn't wandered in at just the right moment. This was only the first of many kindnesses, delivered obliquely but genuinely by our neighbors over the years.

Such generosity, however, doesn't fit the popular image of these people. What passes in the common folklore for Maine character is a near-cynical cantankerousness and wariness of outsiders. And it must be admitted: people from away, especially summer people who care more for their views than for their neighbors, are tolerated but never welcomed as warmly as the money they spend. Even year-round newcomers to a down east community—including Mainers moving from a different part of the

state—can spend years trying to weave themselves into a small town's social fabric and, for all that, they may never truly succeed. In poorer towns especially, unemployment, alcohol, and envy can translate into petty thievery and vandalism against strangers. (Break-ins at vacation cottages and camps are not at all uncommon.)

Overwhelmingly, however, these are a hardworking, honest people possessed of a wry, earthy, and fatalistic wit that's born of their daily struggle to wrest a living from an unforgiving, if beautiful, land and water. (It should never be forgotten that in many of the occupations here, especially those involving the sea, accidental death is a constant if rarely acknowledged companion.) And if the storied Maine aloofness toward outsiders actually exists, it might better be described as an almost shy reserve, hidden by that most rare commodity, good manners.

Urban visitors motoring for the first time down a backwoods road are invariably taken aback when they are greeted by friendly waves of the hand or a simple lift of the fingers off the steering wheel of an approaching vehicle. A city dweller is struck, too, by the lack of status-consciousness among down east people and their neighbors. This is, after all, a state in which any voting member of a community can, with sufficient support, single-handedly alter local budgets or policy in that remarkable relic of direct democracy, the annual town meeting.

Part of this harmony, to be sure, is born of familiarity. In a country where rootlessness is rampant, Maine and its coastal towns harbor families who can trace back their lineage three and four generations in the same place—sometimes even in the same house. Difficult though this might make it for the newcomer to establish roots, such closeness creates a community that nurtures people and tolerates their foibles and failures precisely because they are family. (Of course, as in any family, such closeness can also create tensions, as well as petty jealousies and rivalries.)

Another important unifying factor is race: Maine is more than 98 percent white. What minorities there are, including the state's sizable Native American population, seem to be subject to what one of them has called "a kind of intentional myopia."

"What you suffer from here is a lack of exposure," declares Herb Martin, a former professor at the University of Maine at Machias and, himself, the dark-skinned son of an African-American father and Cherokee mother. Still, Martin says, "there is a kind of refreshing attitude toward survival that I find in Maine, especially when you're in trouble . . . and all that [racist] stuff goes out the window. . . . There are friends here I'll keep forever."

A curious quality about the supposedly gruff Maine character "is a surprising tenderness where it is least expected," writes Martin Dibner in describing the Maine photographs of George Tice. "The men use words like 'love' and 'dear' with a casual frequency that would have worried their Puritan forebears. When I first heard the affectionate terms, it gave me a few uneasy moments: a

carpenter on a construction job sang out to his helper, 'Pass me the power saw, dear, would you now?' and when he got it, he said, 'Now that's a love.'"

Once, after Judy and I sought out a welder in Machias to fashion some metal brackets for our house, she realized in the car on the way home that she had not told him how many we needed. "A bit absentminded, ahn'tcha deah?" he said with a broad smile when she returned red-faced to finish the order.

"It's a mood of sheer joy one gets in Maine with the sun warming one's bones, and green shoots pushing their sprouts through the moist spring earth," Dibner writes. "We do not speak enough with words like 'love' and 'dear'. . . ." At the other seasonal extreme, winters up here are among the most bitter in the country, yet many down-easters say this is their favorite time of year. Why? "Because that's when we get to see each other," one woman told me. "That's when we all can get together for potluck suppers at our neighbors' houses an' keep from goin' stir-crazy." When the roads are warped with frost-heaves and the temperature stays below zero for weeks, it's nice to have company while you wait interminably for first melt.

But even Kenneth Roberts, something of a curmudgeon himself, admitted that he did not love every one of his fellow Mainers, noting that among them were "a number whom I cordially detest, but I like most of them so well that I am proud of being one of them. I like the way they fought the French and Indians, the way they harbored Quakers when Quaker-harboring was a criminal pastime in other parts of the colonies, the way they laughed at Massachusetts witch-hunters when Massachusetts disgraced herself by declaring perpetual open season on those so unfortunate as to be denounced as witches by irresponsibles. . . .

"I particularly like the way her citizens have cast their votes for lost causes which they knew to be right and have only smiled a wintry smile at the misguided jeers of the millions on a bandwagon. The way they refused to admit that to be in a minority is to be wrong."

Sometimes, of course, this independence of will and spirit might seem muddleheaded or foolish. Maine, for example, doesn't require motorcyclists to wear helmets after their first year of operation. Moreover, the state has minimal residential building codes (none of which are observed in the hinterlands) and doesn't require smoke alarms in public buildings unless people sleep there.

"It's not that I'm advocatin' drunk drivin' or anything," one Mainer told me as I made his picture, "but it used to be that if you wanted to drive down the road with a beer in yer hand or keep an old [unregistered] junker to drive back and forth from the store, nobody cared." (Of course, if you lived in certain parts of down east Maine—in the moneyed confines of Hancock Point, Blue Hill, or Northeast Harbor, for instance—they would mind very much.)

In much of Maine, no one seems to care if the piles outside your house or trailer reach proportions that in other, gentler jurisdictions might provoke fines for littering, or even creating a public nuisance. Notes author Carolyn Chute: "Lots of us have assorted useful stuff around our yards—tractors, tractor parts, truck tires, wooden skids, plastic industrial pails, rolled up chicken wire. . . . This comes from freedom, from not worrying what other people think."

In other ways, you are defined here by the sum of your parts—not by what you do but by *how many* things you do to scrape together a living for yourself and your family. The fellow who clears the trees on your property or does the odd carpentry job will also drag for scallops and

sea urchins, and fish for lobster. The woman who bakes pies for a local restaurant will oftentimes fill bait bags for her fisherman husband or boyfriend. And if the dreaded red tide has not closed them down, down east Maine's abundant clam flats—which become visible each day with the prodigious Fundy tide—attract all manner of people for some of the most withering—though profitable—stoop labor imaginable. In these parts, clamming is second only to summer blueberry raking as a source of income earned while bent double.

And come the first frost, everyone is in the evergreen woods, cutting the lush tips from the trees to make Christmas wreaths and garlands.

All this bespeaks a rugged and simpler lifestyle, one that to a large extent still exists—even if the favorite evening's entertainment has shifted from reading quietly by a fire or playing the fiddle or guitar to watching videos rented from the convenience store down the road.

Consider that:

Until only a few years ago, residents of Lubec could dial their neighbors using only the last four digits of their phone numbers. The last time residents of New York City could do this was in March 1940.

Though cable and satellite dishes provide multi-channel TV viewing, radio reception down east is, at best, a some-time thing. Riding along Route One between Whiting and Machias, you can play a funny kind of roulette with the car radio. Press the "scan" button most times during the day, and you will get a single AM station and a single FM station. The rest will be static.

The local down east papers—weeklies and biweeklies, of course—are throwbacks to a time when news was provided largely by volunteers, not paid staff. For example, a while back, the *Machias Valley News Observer* provided the news from Cutler in the form of a report from Mrs. Glenn Farris. It began as follows: "We have had here in Cutler only two very hot days, so far. . . ." Over in Eastport, the *Quoddy Tides* entertains its readers with features like "Book Nook by Bea" and "Outdoors with Ed." Nancy and Fred Hastings, editors of the excellent *Downeast Coastal Press*, do final paste-up and copy editing in a tiny office near their home in Cutler, within a few yards of their livestock. And the *Lubec Light,* a monthly, once featured a cooking column by Gloria Christie, a native Mainer who made her pies, breads, baked beans, and fish chowders on a wood-burning stove in her tin-roofed kitchen.

This is not to say that people here embrace the simple life in the way that the well-to-do rusticators of the 1870s did, in self-conscious, back-to-nature summers that ended each fall when they resumed their well-padded lives in New York, Boston, and other points south. Nor does it mean that the region is immune to change—only that progress ventures up the coast with a ponderous and blessed slowness. The people of down east Maine who are pictured here live this way because they have to. That they *want* to, as well, is what makes them and this place so unusual.

FRANK VAN RIPER
Lubec, Maine
July 1998

T W O - R O O M   S C H O O L H O U S E

They arrive fresh-faced and scrubbed on a sunlit morning in early September, with the same mixture of anticipation and dread that children everywhere feel on the first day of school. In the small down east Maine community of Whiting, the bus pulls up to the white clapboard schoolhouse at eight A.M. sharp.

Just one bus and a scattering of cars. Total enrollment: thirty-six.

The Whiting Village School was built in 1825 and served as a one-room school through much of its early life, providing public education for the children of the farmers and fishermen who lived in the surrounding villages of Washington County. Eventually, as the region grew, Whiting expanded into a two-room school, with kindergarten through fourth grade in one room, fifth grade through eighth in the other.

The potbellied stove that warmed teacher and charges in earlier years (the job of tending the stove was assigned to a reliable student) eventually gave way to a more modern heating system. There's a computer lab now, tucked into one corner of the building, near the copying machine. Still, with its weathered wood floors, tin ceilings, hand-cranked pencil sharpener, and ancient slate blackboards, the Whiting Village School retains the look—and, more important, the atmosphere—of schools that have all but disappeared from other parts of the country.

"The advantage is that the older kids can help the little kids," says the principal, Pauline Cates, who teaches the upper grades. An educator for thirty-four years, the last twelve at Whiting, Cates speaks with obvious affection about a school that, on a meager budget, has retained both excellence and pride in learning. Though most of Whiting's three dozen children live in the area, a few "tuition" students come from nearby Trescott, an "unorganized territory" with no school of its own. "Their parents have applied to the state to allow them to come here, and the state pays their tuition," Cates explains.

And more than one pupil comes from hard-pressed Lubec, whose consolidated school, just a few miles away, seems always beset with the kind of staffing and discipline problems associated with larger systems. Lubec families have been known to move down the road simply to place children within Whiting's jurisdiction.

On this first day of class, there are special chores that the older children set to with vigor, while the younger ones—especially the five-year-old first-timers (who are overwhelmed by it all)—sit quietly at their desks. There is much stapling and taping of construction paper to walls and bulletin boards. Desks and chairs have to be selected, by size and height. And though Cates and Charlene Myers, who teaches the lower grades, know everyone by sight, attendance has to be taken.

By mid-morning, both classrooms are ready, and Whiting's thirty-six students settle into their desks.

"Some of you who are talking need to be reminded that you shouldn't be," Cates says in a firm, quiet voice. Now textbooks are allotted, reading assignments given, and projects described. Within a short time, the two classrooms settle into an orderly hum, the just-ended summer only a memory.

THE LAST FAIR OF SUMMER

Nervously, but also with pride, the young boy lifts his lop-eared bunny onto the table. With some prompting from the pigtailed judge, he answers all the questions about how he raised the animal—what he fed it, the steps he took to keep it healthy, and so on.

At the woman's urging, the boy turns the animal over on its back, trying to keep it from wiggling off the table as the judge inspects its paws and underside. When the woman is done, the child hefts the rabbit into his arms and places it gently back in its carrier. Then he leaves the arena—to the warm applause of the crowd—as another child and another rabbit prepare to face the judge.

Nearby, the oxen pull goes on with equal seriousness but considerably more drama. In double teams, the huge beasts strain to the shouted commands of their whip-wielding handlers, the oxen dragging immense cement blocks back and forth across the dusty infield. They race the clock amid the noise of the crowd, their large, liquid eyes bulging with the effort.

The air is thick with music and the smells of animals and fried dough. Joie Chitwood is running his thrills-and-spills car show in the main arena, while the 4-H exhibition in a nearby pavilion features squash and pumpkins of gargantuan size and variety. The midway is awash in games, souvenirs, and rides.

The lengthening shadows of late afternoon signal the end of summer, and the Blue Hill Fair, as it has for generations, heralds the arrival of fall.

A fair, any fair, is a gathering of clans: a place to meet friends, renew acquaintances, and show off one's animals, crops, or skills. It is also a place to eat any number of things that are bad for you.

Like its counterpart in Union or like the Blueberry Festival farther east, in Machias, the Blue Hill Fair is a summer tradition. This year is no exception, the only change being the cancellation of the end-of-fair fireworks because of an unusually dry summer.

For four days and nights over the Labor Day weekend, people by the thousands stream through the fairground gates led by their kids, who race to the rides and the food stands, anxious for one last fling before the start of school

only a few days away. This is no time for moderation; brisk business at the Road Kill pizza stand, the fried-dough and onion-ring booths, the Italian sausage stands, as well as the blueberry cobbler booth, all attest to that.

If some animals work during the fair—the oxen, as well as the muscular horses that also pull great loads in competition—other creatures display their excellence in dignified silence. A pair of champion cows, their dappled hides making a pleasant counterpoint to the striped tent that houses them, rest quietly on a bed of straw. Their owners sit beside them in folding chairs, chatting amiably with the passersby, who marvel at the cows' elegance and mass. So, too, do prize goats and sheep pass the time—in (relative) silence, huddled in pens in open-sided barns. (The ducks, chickens, and geese, however, receive their admirers with noise.)

Perhaps most active are the sheepdogs, whose handlers run them through an intricate program before a cheering grandstand as the dogs try—at times with only moderate success—to herd sheep from one end of the infield to the other, over a wooden bridge, through a gate, and finally into a holding pen. The dogs respond to shouted and whistled commands, and the best of them fairly burst with the desire to bring sheep to heel. Some dogs' eagerness to get on with their business is comical—they crawl stealthily on their bellies toward the nervous woolies, in the manner of Wile E. Coyote tracking the never-to-be-outdone Road Runner.

Halfway through the fair, on a sunny, unseasonably warm September afternoon, the blueberry-pie-eating contest is held on the same platform from which trophies were earlier awarded the owners of the winning sheepdogs. In teams of four, boys and girls selected at random from prospective entries, troop to the stage to be cloaked in plastic garbage bags, only their heads showing through. The rules require that no hands be used, and at the shouted "Go!" they dive gustily and face first into the goo. One boy—he's probably been here before—looks up occasionally, just long enough to eye his competition. Then he careens back into the blue, right up to his eyes. He is a wiry kid, but he beats out the beefier boy two spaces down. In the end there is pie everywhere—on faces, up noses, in hair. The winners get trophies, much like those given the sheepdogs.

A spectacular crimson sky covers the fairgrounds as day turns to evening, and the brilliant, dappled mixture of reds and blues gives a gentle backdrop to the confusion and noise of the midway. The carnival lights of the roulette booths, the dart-throws, the ball-tosses, and all the other games that shout for one's money become more garish as day turns to night.

The rides, especially the ones that go fast and spin wildly, become more exciting, the enveloping darkness making them seem more titillating and dangerous. Not so the snub-nosed, wheel-less bumper cars. Tethered to an electric roof by a long metal rod and doomed to move slowly regardless of the driver, they remain as sweet-natured and approachable as ever.

W O R K I N G   T H E   T I D E

Only blueberry raking matches it for back-breaking toil.

Clamming—digging for soft-shelled clams in unyielding wet clay with a short, heavy clam rake—is one of the toughest ways to harvest seafood because it is done by hand, a few clams at a time. And it can't be done in water.

Clammers watch the tide tables as assiduously as lobstermen. Only, unlike the fishermen, the clammers wait for dead low tide, when coves are turned into mudflats thanks to the amazing pull of the Bay of Fundy. (They also watch for, and respect, warnings of red tide; the plankton-produced toxin can temporarily make clams and quahogs that have fed on it poisonous, if not deadly.)

When the water drops, be it in cool fog or under a hot sun, the high rubber boots go on and the clammers wade ponderously into the flats, searching for the telltale blowholes in the mud, indicating that clams are lurking beneath the surface. A good day of digging can yield several baskets of clams, which then are sold, mostly to local restaurants or stores.

Every summer, one can count on seeing a tourist who is taken with the idea of clamming for his or her evening meal. One also can count on that tourist quickly tiring of the game and heading for the local takeout stand for a mess of juicy, sweet fried clams that, likely as not, were harvested hours before—by somebody else.

HUNTING THE BLACK SHADOW

Ask anyone who has lost livestock to them, much less a footrace: black bears are a fact of life in Maine. Smaller and less aggressive than the great grizzlies of the west, these New England natives nevertheless can be fierce when threatened—possessed of razor-sharp claws, unbelievable strength, and surprising speed. Moreover, they are everywhere; cubs often show up as road kill and are occasionally mounted by taxidermists.

Full grown, black bears are, in the words of one Maine guide, "killing machines," and only a fool or a romantic will venture into the woods unawares. But they are gentle creatures, too, generally skittish and wary of humans to the point of running at the first sniff of them. At the same time, however, the bears find irresistible the stuff humans eat or throw away.

They can be maddening nuisances. Scavengers of garbage and livestock, they have been known to brazenly root through vehicles, tents, and chicken coops. Jim Honnell of Cardville, Maine, recalls how one 300-pound black bear that he named "Chico" made a practice of dining from the pickup truck full of stale pastries that Honnell used to feed his pigs. In a matter of weeks, Honnell says, other bears joined Chico, appearing every day and at all hours—just yards from Honnell's trailer home. By mid-July—six weeks before it would have been legal to shoot them—the bears were so prevalent that Honnell, his wife, and his two kids were virtual captives.

Hunting bear in Maine can be a lucrative business for professional guides, who, in the weeks before hunting season, carefully tend their bait sites. They lard each one with donuts, molasses, cereal, chicken legs, and other items, the better to guarantee a steady stream of bears, quick kills—and satisfied clients.

It is easy to view this kind of hunting as a one-sided exercise favoring beer-guzzling men dressed in camo suits and armed with high-powered rifles, men who hunger for nothing more than a trophy for the wall. But that is not even half right. It ignores the simple reality that bear hunting is, for the vast majority of Maine hunters—both men and women—a way to provide food for the winter, as well as the most efficient means to thin a wild population that, left unchecked, would inevitably threaten humans.

A challenging contest between human and bear, it is sport, one that excites the senses and that creates in the young a lifetime bond with woods and family. It is a contest, to be sure, but one that the bear, not the hunter, most often wins.

"I think I told you my 'bear feeder' theory," writes Randy Cross, a field biologist for Maine's Department of Inland Fisheries and Wildlife. He hunts bear with his family in late summer every year—six months after he and his colleagues use snowmobiles and snowshoes to help monitor and count the bear population and tag the newly born cubs. "As people feed birds and watch them out the window, we do the same with bears." In a typical year, Cross estimates

that he and his family put out literally thousands of pounds of feed at their dozen bait sites, feed that sustains not only bears and their young but "all of their woodsmates as well, including ravens, squirrels, martens, mice, coyotes, raccoons, rabbits, porcupines, Canada jays and other birds."

It is the bears' silence and cunning, even more than their strength or speed, that makes them so difficult to hunt. "The Indians called them the Black Shadow," says Randy's brother, Art, as he makes the rounds of his bait sites. He fills plastic garbage bags to near-bursting with a mixture of molasses, grains, and used Fryolator grease—a bear delicacy—then strings them from trees where they hang tantalizingly. Twenty yards away, high in the branches, is the hunting platform where Art, Randy, their father (Arthur), or any of the hunters that accompany them will wait.

The rule is one person to a stand at each bait site; there the hunter must sit motionless and quiet—fearing even to clear the throat lest he spook a hungry bear into flight. The bait sites are tended in late August or early September during the heat of the day, when the bears are resting. The hunters climb the platforms at dusk—feeding time—then try their best to become one with the forest, waiting for a bear to emerge, often in such total and eerie silence that it seems simply to materialize.

The wait can last hours, often yielding no bears at all. Yet the woods are alive at this time, and the show is worth it. All sorts of animals range over the pickings that have been laid out by the hunters, and the hunters—especially those who love and appreciate what they are seeing—speak of this time with a fascination bordering on reverence.

To lengthen the odds even more, Randy and his father hunt with muzzle-loading rifles, meaning that they have only one shot to make a kill. They carry "quick-loads" with pre-measured amounts of black powder, but, in fact, the success or failure of a day's hunt depends on that first lead ball and the hunter's ability to make a clean shot while his heart pounds like a trip hammer and adrenaline surges through his body.

As noted, the odds favor the bear, which is fine with Randy and his relatives. They look forward to the annual hunt as a family gathering, a ritual filled with tradition and campfire stories of the ones that got away, as much as tales of the ones that didn't. "I think our bear hunts can be summed up by a phrase I've heard applied to different cases," Randy says: "'In a world that's going 90 miles per hour, it's our way of putting on the brakes.'"

On one day in late August, Randy's father spied but a single bear—a sow with her cubs—and held his fire. Minutes later, from Randy's site, the woods exploded with the huge report of his muzzle-loader. But the shot went wide, and the bear ran off.

Before the Labor Day weekend was over that season, Randy reported that his brother, their father, and "a fella from Florida we nicknamed 'Grits' for CB purposes," all bagged their limit (one bear per hunter per season).

Still, with the possible exception of Grits, one senses that if they had come up empty again, it would not have mattered.

KING OF BANGOR

He can suffer the occasional dismissal of his work by critics. Having more books in print than anyone else, save perhaps William Shakespeare, can lessen the sting of any scribbler's slings and arrows.

What hurts are the casual cruelties, says Stephen King, sitting in the anonymous, unmarked suite of offices he maintains in an industrial park near the Bangor airport. "I was here at the office the other day, and there was a guy came up from International Paper next door, and he wanted an autograph for his wife."

King obliged the man, who probably didn't know how lucky he was. (There is now hardly any such thing as a Stephen King book signing—the crowds would simply be unmanageable.)

Standing in King's office, the man from International Paper made it clear he only was there at his wife's behest.

"Frankly, I never read that kind of stuff myself," he said.

"What kind of stuff are you talking about," King asked.

"Oh, that horror stuff."

"Well, you know," King responded, "I've written love stories, like *The Dead Zone*, and I've written straight suspense, and I've written some stuff that doesn't have anything to do with horror or the supernatural at all.

"And this man's kind of like noddin' along and saying 'Well, if I ever decide I wanna try a horror story. . . .'

"So what I'm saying," King laments, "is they don't hear you."

Although he makes no apology for the buckets of blood he has thrown across the deck over the last twenty years, he would like to be remembered for more.

"Let's put it this way," King says with a hesitant laugh, "if you were a girl and you turned tricks to support yourself when you were, say, twenty-one or twenty-two years old, would it be fair to still call you a whore if you were forty-eight or forty-nine years old and a respectable person?

"I'm gonna be 'the master of the modern horror story' until I die. Even if what I write turns to drivel, they will still call me the master of the modern horror story."

But the writing hasn't turned to drivel. A man of uncommon narrative gifts, King, at fifty, is a literary phenomenon. He has written successfully—and well—in many genres, including science fiction, fantasy, suspense, the short story, the "serial thriller," the novella, and even—in the case of *Dolores Claiborne*—first-person narration. Hence he is difficult, if not impossible, to pigeonhole.

He is the rare writer who is both a storyteller and chameleon, able to adopt different styles seemingly at will. Driven to write, he does so virtually every day, on everything from a computer to a steno pad. There's nothing new or special about writers who are, in effect, writing machines. Most, though, are hacks. But King is special: he is a writing machine with talent—as well as wit, grace, and—every so often—a nasty streak that can rob you of a night's sleep.

His wife, Tabitha, is also a best-selling novelist, as well as King's staunchest defender. A short, pugnacious woman with a brilliant smile and dark horn-rimmed glasses, she dismisses critics who think that her husband "must be writing shit because he sells too many copies." Then, she says, they actually read the books, find that they can't stop reading them, discover good things in them, and "fight it all the way!"

With the fame and wealth that derives from two decades of bestsellers, Stephen King, Tabitha, and their three children could live anywhere. But they choose to stay in the working-class city of Bangor.

"It's home," King says, "and the kids, I guess, hold us to it. [Son] Owen went to high school here. Obviously we have a lot of interests in the community and we have friends here. Let's face it, it's the source of our material."

It is also the place that nurtured them during the hard times, when King was struggling as an English teacher, when Tabitha was holding down assorted jobs to keep their young family fed. Understandably, then, it is a place and a region to which King and his wife feel both a bond and an obligation. Their acts of charity and kindness to local people and institutions go largely unheralded now, though it was impossible to keep quiet the more than $1 million that the Kings donated to the construction of the senior little league field in Bangor, where Stephen—a baseball nut—has on occasion coached.

"I tell you something," he says. "If you get a certain amount of celebrity, if you get well known, it's nice to be with people who know you for who you really are. It keeps your feet on the ground . . . and when they talk to you they're not talking to a celebrity, they're talkin' to Steve and Tabby up the street."

But celebrity can take a toll—even in Bangor—in the form of the damaged and deranged who are attracted to the famous like moths to a flame. For several years, a man claiming King was the real killer of singer John Lennon cruised Bangor in a van decked with signs accusing the writer of the murder. Given such incidents, one can accept the unlisted phone number, the anonymous office, and the protective staff—even in a town that views King and his wife not merely as friends, but as family.

The craft of writing is solitary. It still happens—and always will—one word at a time. That suits King, who probably prefers to think of himself as a craftsman. He almost never outlines the books he writes—even if they wind up inches thick and several pounds heavy. "When you outline a book it's like going on a train, on tracks that have been laid," he says. "When you don't outline, it's like being on a hovercraft. You can go all over the desert if you want."

Legwork and research? "I do most of it myself," says King. "I have to go talk to a guy in New York next month . . . about ways of stealing credit from credit cards. I could get somebody else to do a report or something like that, but it seems to stick better a lot of times if you do it yourself; the questions that you ask go to the heart of the matter.

"The one thing about writing, it doesn't change from century to century. It's still hand work."

D E E P - W A T E R P O R T

For a state with some twenty-five hundred miles of irregular coastline, Maine has surprisingly few harbors that can accommodate deep-draft shipping. Eastport, which sits right on the border with Canada, is one of the busiest, handling both domestic and international cargo.

THE OLDEST POSTMASTER

Albert Mahar, postmaster of the tiny town of Dennysville, tells his story while leaning against a battered metal table, a wooden nest of pigeonholes behind him. Crowned by neatly cropped snow-white hair, his smooth face falls easily into a smile as he speaks.

There's a lull this afternoon; most of the town's residents picked up their mail earlier in the day or had it delivered to their RFD mailboxes. The postal truck that will take the small basket of outgoing mail to Brewer isn't due until four. That's a half-hour before Albert will lock his door for the day and head home to his wife Mary, to the house that sits across the town's one main road, within sight of the Dennys River, where he once loved to fish.

With more than sixty years' work under his belt, Mahar holds the record for the longest continuous service of any U.S. postmaster, and at eighty-five, he is the oldest postmaster in the country. He now serves the great-grandchildren of his original customers.

One might argue that Mahar took the first steps on his road to longevity when he got lost in New York's Grand Central Station in 1927. He had hoped to follow his two sisters to a steady teaching position in Long Branch, New Jersey, south of New York. They had sent him a train ticket to get him to New York for an interview, and they had told him to wait under the clock at Grand Central until one of them picked him up. It took more than two hours of mixed signals—Albert was standing under the wrong clock—for brother and sister to hook up.

After only two days, Mahar knew the big city was not for him. The bustle, the noise—even the food and the air—seemed alien. Finally, he told his sisters: "If you'll give me train fare back to that wide place in the road, I'm on my way."

For the next five years—in the midst of the Great Depression—Mahar taught seventh and eighth grade in Machias and had a chance to teach high school. But over the years, his salary didn't increase; it actually fell. "I could see that I was getting ahead no better fast.

"Well, my father was a Democrat . . . and I said I might as well jump on the bandwagon and listen to 'em." That timely move—at the start of the Roosevelt era—served Mahar well when the job of Dennysville postmaster came open. One of oldtime politics' prime local patronage plums, the spot went to Mahar because he was a Democrat. The salary was $1,000 a year, twice what he was making as a teacher.

That was February 1, 1935, when stamps cost three cents and when the local carrier delivered letters by horse and wagon—or horse and sleigh in winter. Except for four years in the army during World War II, Mahar hasn't hung his hat anywhere else but in Dennysville, a place that never had more than one main road—and likely never will.

A Small-Town Fourth

The music comes from a handful of people sitting on folding chairs by the side of the road. The "floats" are homemade, tiny, and pulled by all-terrain vehicles. A lone American flag hangs across the town's main road and flaps lazily in the morning breeze coming off the harbor.

Typical of the region, Fourth of July in Cutler is more a day-long gathering of families and friends than a high-decibel exercise of public patriotism. The Kids' Parade is a low-key walk down main street, parents accompanying children on tricycles. Boy Scouts and Girl Scouts march smartly in their uniforms, and a color guard from the nearby naval station provides an escort for Neil Corbett, a septuagenarian lobsterman who, as the parade's grand marshal, waves to all from a horse-drawn buggy.

Before the parade, townspeople parked themselves on neighbors' lawns and chatted amiably in the welcome sun, which finally decided to show after several days of rain. There were no hawkers selling souvenirs along the parade route, no police barricades holding back the crowd.

Willard Scott was nowhere in sight as the parade got underway.

Among the floats, the one patriotic effort is a near-life-size replica of the Liberty Bell—or as close as one could get with aluminum foil and a black felt-tip marker. It is escorted by children wearing tricornered hats made of paper and Colonial wigs looking suspiciously like floor mops. There are kids dressed as come-alive sunflowers and cartoon characters, and there is at least one small Superman.

After the parade, everyone walks up the road to the town's ballfield. The penny scramble is soon to come, but not before the soda-drinking contest.

Every activity this day is locally sponsored and financed. The noon "turkey dinner with all the fixings" is underwritten by Cutler United Methodist Women. During the soda-drinking contest, the hat is passed to pay for the sodas for next year. The community picnic at the ballfield is also locally done: the free hot dogs, hamburgers, and drinks are paid for by area businesses, and prepared and served by volunteers.

In a coastal town like Cutler, where many people make their living on the water, it is natural that there be "water games" like lobster crate races and canoe races. But these are only a prelude to the main event: the annual competition among Cutler's lobsterboats, when the doughty vessels, built for stability not speed, have their one chance all year to cut loose. Now their captains ride the throttle full open, and no one worries about hauling hundreds of traps and miles of pot warp.

At day's end, a starry night sky cloaks Cutler Harbor. Workboats at anchor punctuate the water in the gathering dark as, in the distance, men move nimbly onto a barge to ready the fireworks. The first Cutler has ever had, they are being paid for by a year of bottle drives and other homegrown financing. Every so often, a signal flare goes up from nearby workboats, and for a while it appears that these will be all the pyrotechnics for the evening. The shouts and laughter that carry over the still water make it obvious even to anxious spectators that young pranksters out in the harbor are delighting in capturing the crowd's attention, if only for a moment.

Suddenly the night sky explodes, and for the next half-hour the tiny town of Cutler celebrates Independence Day in high, exuberant style worthy of any town's glorious Fourth.

"M A K E   A   S T A R T   F O R   G O D"

There are mosquitoes in the air this cool July evening, and there is joyful noise as well. The Holy Ghost is among the faithful, and many rise up in prayerful ecstasy. Backed by drums and keyboard, the Reverend A. C. Calhoun is beginning the second night of his three-day tent revival in a wide, open field on the outskirts of Lubec.

"Praise Jesus! Praise God!" the preacher says over and over, and the arriving crowd murmurs with him, in time to the chords from the electric organ. "Grab your neighbor's hand—some of you young people, that's a chance you been wantin' for a long time!—and let's lift our voices and ask that God will give us a miracle here tonight. . . ."

Suddenly Calhoun begins speaking in tongues, and a woman in the crowd stands and responds in kind.

"Hallelujah! Hallelujah!"

The departing sun has turned the sky crimson as the last cars pull up and park by the nearby VFW Post. "Tent Crusade Here!!!—We Welcome You" says a hand-lettered wooden sign nailed to a telephone pole at the edge of the field, near Route 189.

The yellow-and-white-striped tent is hard to miss from the road. Inside, men and women, many holding tightly to their well-thumbed Bibles, fill the seventy-five folding chairs that face a plain wooden platform. On it stands an ornately carved wooden pulpit where Calhoun, a young man of perhaps thirty-five with a large head, horn-rimmed glasses, and a shiny gray suit, raises his arms in exultation over what is to come. There's going to be a miracle here tonight; he can feel it.

Calhoun is pastor of the United Pentecostal Church at Wilson's Beach, Campobello. He and his wife are sponsors of the three-day revival, along with the Pentecostal Church of East Machias. But for all his exuberance, Calhoun is just the warm-up for the main event: an evening of pulpit-pounding, stem-winding, and salvation delivered by Reverend Rick Stoops of Augusta, Maine, a Pentecostal preacher who collects souls with the intensity of an old-time gunfighter gathering notches on his pistol.

A burly man who, like Calhoun, favors shiny gray shark-skin, Stoops towers over many in his flock. He has curly black hair, a soft-jowled face, and an intense stare. Though he and his wife have lived in Maine for nearly two decades, his voice retains the soft drawl of his native Midwest. When he jabs the air or suddenly puts a harmonica to his mouth for "This Train is Bound for Glory," the picture instantly ages a half-century, back to the days of Wendell Willkie and Huey Long, great political tub-thumpers whose speeches were as much performance as oration.

The Reverend A. C. Calhoun was the youngest of five children, and by the time he was born, all the members of his family had become Pentecostals—baptized by immersion and touched by God, they believed in the literal teachings of the Bible. Others might be "born again," Stoops says before the service (in a whisper, so he can save his voice), "but that may mean many things. You can say, 'I accept the Lord Jesus as my personal savior' or 'I signed the church register' or 'I laid my hand on the television set' but all of those things absolutely have nothing whatsoever to do with what the Bible says about being born again."

It is an article of faith to Pentecostals that, in order to enjoy eternal salvation, one must go down to the river. "He that believeth and is baptized shall be saved," Stoops intones to his flock this evening as he takes the pulpit, "but he that believeth not shall be damned." More than anything, Stoops, Calhoun, and the other church people want to walk to the water—in this case, Lubec Harbor—and baptize all comers in the chill evening air. Tonight, however, it will be a hard sell.

"I would love to have the opportunity to pray for you in the name of the Lord Jesus Christ," Stoops says, beginning in a low rumble. "I'd love to see the name of Jesus get exalted in Lubec tonight." His voice rises ever so slightly as the electric organ paces him with random soothing chords.

Then, fixing the crowd with his stare: "I want every Christian to realize the power that's invested in you! When you begin to use the name of Jesus Christ in sincerity and in holiness—when you call upon that name—demons tremble and angels come to your beckon!

Finally, in near shout: "I tell you there's POWER in the name of Jesus!"

"Amen!" "Praise Jesus!" come the responses.

For the better part of an hour, Stoops goes nonstop, in roller coaster cadences that build in extremes of shudder and shout. "Friends," Stoops says, staring intently into the crowd, "if I was not baptized in Jesus' name, I would not go to sleep tonight before I said, 'Preacher, baptize me.'"

But no one stands to accept the call.

"You can talk in tongues all you want, Ma'am," an exasperated Stoops tells one standing, clapping woman, "but you gotta be baptized in Jesus' name! Same goes for you, sir."

Still no takers.

Finally, Stoops is reduced to asking, "How many will come forward and say I will firmly consider this?"

There is a slight stirring in the crowd but hardly the rush forward that Stoops and the others wanted.

The miracle of salvation will have to wait. The organist segues into a mournful hymn, and the congregation joins Stoops in song as he winds up the prayer meeting.

"Would you do this?" he asks. "Would you pray for the person next to you?" He asks all to "make a start for God," for each to implore the Lord, "cleanse my heart, Jesus."

It is dark now, the chill evening air driving away the mosquitoes, as Stoops, Calhoun, and the others leave the pulpit and wade into the crowd for individual prayer and counsel. Slowly they make their way among those seeking them, stopping now and then to embrace someone, to take his or her head in their hands, and to ask God's blessing.

It is this image that lingers: Stoops lost in prayer, his eyes shut, hands clasped tightly to the head of a young girl in a black leather jacket. The rest of the ministers, standing to the side, offering their touch and their intensity, form a tableau of faith that is frozen by the camera's flash and a lone naked lightbulb.

Make a start. In the end, that is all one can ask.

ONE TENT, THREE RINGS

Dawn greets the big top. Hoisted up at sun's first light, the striped tent that houses the Roberts' Bros. Circus dominates the old fairgrounds across from the Down East Community Hospital, on the outskirts of Machias. The yards of canvas and the hundreds of slats, poles, ropes, rings, and other paraphernalia that make up a circus wear the weathered look of more than twenty years' hard use. This equipment moves up and down the East Coast, from Florida to Maine and back again, from March to October each year—a different town every day.

"You can't compare Ringling with this circus," says James Allen, a burly, bare-chested roustabout who also mans the concession stand—and who occasionally assists the clowns. "Now, Ringling [The Ringling Bros. and Barnum & Bailey Circus—The Greatest Show on Earth], they play in an auditorium, and you can't get personal with no one. You can't see anything. Here, you can sit anywhere in our big top, and you can see the whole show."

Barely a generation ago, more than a hundred of these one-tent shows were playing small towns all across rural America. Now there are maybe a dozen.

To go to a tent circus—to smell the peanuts, to watch the children watching the clowns, to hear the calliope, to see a show whose most exotic animal is one tiny elephant—is to go back in time. This is the world before television, before video games, before the hollow thrill of virtual reality.

Still, any circus, even a small one like this, is a maze of its own moving parts that must be assembled and taken down with each new town. Everyone associated with it has several jobs that must be done long before the first ticket is sold.

As the morning sun grows hotter, James and the dozen or so other young men who make up the ground crew work methodically. With the tent finally up, they pound into the ground the long steel rods that will support the platforms and wires of the aerialists. Then the crew will assemble the three wooden rings that will encircle, if not the Greatest Show on Earth, then a miniature version of it.

An earnest fellow who wears a bandanna on his head and puffs continuously on a corncob pipe, says he is from Maine, his hometown just seventy miles from Machias.

"This is totally different from any other job you can have," he declares. "You do a different thing every day.

"Why join the circus? Well, what got me to join is I was unemployed," he says with a laugh. "We're what you call roustabouts."

"That's what in the music business you'd call a roadie," chimes in one of his partners, amid the music of sledge striking steel.

"Each person has different reasons why they joined. Some is unemployment. Some is trying to get away from things. But like I said, this job is totally different from any job you could ever, *ever* think of.

"Roustabouts sometimes get a bad rap—but we're not carneys [people who work at carnivals and midways]. Carney people and circus people are two different kinds. Carney people are rude, arrogant, and obnoxious. But in the circus, we have to treat people with the utmost respect, and we have to

treat them like people, not like marks or pigeons. If you treat 'em like that, they ain't comin' back."

"We have repeat customers," James Allen interjects. Every year, we come back and there are people who remember us from the previous year. And generally we like to change the routine of the show—this year we have a whole new show."

Like what?

"Well, there's no high-wire act this year, but we do have a great aerial display—three rings of aerials. We have a balancing act in the center of the ring and two cradle acts on the end rings. . . .

"Tequila is our horse," continues Allen. "And we have three liberty ponies, potbellied pigs, two performing goats—and llamas." (For the record, there are also jugglers, performing dogs, and Lisa, the main attraction. She is a 7,000-pound Asian elephant who earns her keep before the show by giving rides to kids.)

"We have two clowns, Roddo and Bucky. And I myself participate in one of the gags," James notes proudly. "We have a boxing gag that we do, and I'm the referee."

"I'm inside all the time," he says. "I do the inside concession stand. Sometimes I'm in a mood to watch the show, and other times I'm not in the mood, but I do know what's going on."

The roustabouts are a varied lot, including some individuals who have clearly seen better times. But the Roberts' Bros. show is a family-run affair, and it appears that the management takes a paternal interest in its people. "Some of the other shows, they pay you more," says James, "but you have to pay for your room and board and meals. In this show, room and board is provided, plus you get money to spend." (Later one of the roustabouts

concedes the reason spending money is parceled out each day is to keep some from blowing a week's wages in one night.)

By mid-afternoon, the big top is ready. There are two shows this evening, at five-thirty and seven-thirty, with a portion of the gate earmarked for a local charity. The crowds come early.

"Ladieeeees and gentlemen—and children of all ages," comes the hoary yet stirring opening cry from ringmaster (and show manager) Jeffrey Earl. A handsome man with a worried brow and dark mustache, Earl is the picture of every circus ringmaster in his wing collar and bright red tailcoat. His amplified voice booms through the ancient tent, and the hundreds of people who crowd the worn bleachers settle in for the show.

"When you get a bag of peanuts, look inside," Earl intones. "There might be a ticket there and if there is, bring it to Mr. Smith there. [Mr. Smith, who hours earlier was pounding tent poles, waves and smiles.] He will give you one of those beautiful balloons he is holding—ab-so-lutely free!

"Delicious, dry-roasted in the shell, oldtime circus peanuts. Just one dollar a bag."

The show goes off with admirable precision, the recorded music cutting off in mid-note each time Earl raises the microphone to his lips to announce the next act. The jugglers juggle, the aerialists fly through the air, the potbellied pigs scamper around the center ring, Lisa the elephant holds all in her thrall, and the earnest performing dogs act as if their very being depends on getting through their act without mishap.

The show ends with a patriotic tableau featuring a huge American flag that is hung from the center of the big top. Eve-

ning air, with just the hint of approaching fall, greets the departing crowd. When the great tent is empty, James Allen, Mr. Smith, and the rest of the crew, who earlier had been hawking balloons and selling peanuts, set to work once more to bring down the big top and pack it away.

Another town, another show.

Until next year.

THE PERILOUS ART OF LOBSTERING

The collection cans were in the local convenience stores within days after the *Joanie Lynne* was discovered adrift and unmanned off Moosabec Reach. A search by sea and air yielded only a glove and a cap. Within a week the family had placed the obituary in the papers. Lobsterman Milton Anthony, fifty-five, was lost at sea July 29, 1996, and was presumed drowned. His intact body was never recovered.

Lobstering is often seen as a romantic occupation, conjuring up images of stoic, independent sailors hauling traps from a rolling sea, harvesting creatures that in centuries past were so plentiful they littered the beaches. But this is dangerous work, and a year rarely passes that at least one Maine lobsterman doesn't lose his life in the unforgiving, fatally cold water.

Part of the danger is in the process itself. *Homarus americanus*—the native lobster so identified with Maine that for years it adorned the state's license plates—is a secretive thing, preferring to scavenge for food in the deepest, coldest waters. It must be enticed into bulky traps that need to be tended religiously, and the routine is unforgiving: Each pot must be checked regardless of its contents, so that bait can be replaced. Even a trap full of lobsters—three or four— cannot be left for another day. Lobsters are cannibals, and overcrowding will invariably cause one or two to be killed and eaten by their own.

So the process goes on, day in, day out.

Every year, there is concern that the number of lobsters is dwindling, that this great natural resource, which—in many ways—defines coastal Maine, will fall victim to overfishing, much like the famed blue crabs of the Chesapeake Bay.

The dilemma is ripe for controversy. On one side are the "fishcrats"—politicians in the state capital of Augusta— armed with scientific studies that invariably endorse limiting the lobster catch as a means to conserve what scientists see as a finite resource.

On the other side are the lobstermen, loosely organized yet vociferous. They claim, with justification, that previous conservation efforts have done nothing but cost them money. They also note that, like the blue crab, the lobster exhibits a maddening tendency to appear in huge numbers nearly every time some expert from the state has sounded the species' death knell.

It's no wonder a lobsterman's favorite place is by himself, in his boat, away from the madding noise of Augusta and, by extension, civilization. To watch a two-person lobstering team—captain and sternman—bringing up pot after pot as dawn breaks over the cold inshore waters is to watch an ancient unchanging ballet.

In the chill predawn there is little need for conversation between David Lord and his father, Paul, as the two men board a tiny dinghy in a sheltered cove in north Lubec. It will bring them to their lobsterboat, sitting at anchor a few hundred yards distant. A half hour's ride in the pitching sea off Quoddy Head, and they are among the hundred or so traps whose location is marked by bobbing buoys that bear their mark. Each buoy is attached to a submerged lobster pot by a length of stout pot warp, and each pot must be tended by hand.

With practiced skill, David maneuvers the boat alongside a buoy, then takes the engine out of gear. With a long-handled gaff he snares the buoy and brings it on board, deftly placing its slippery rope into the grip of the hydraulic winch—a concession to modern technology that will do the hauling. Once the trap breaks the water's skin, David grabs it and, with a slight roll of his hips, hauls it on board, searching its contents for the elusive lobster. There are lobsters this day, though not as many as David and Paul had hoped. But then, no lobsterman likes even a single empty trap, much less one filled with trash fish and sea urchins.

Every lobsterman carries with him a brass gauge to measure the carapace, or main body shell, of every lobster taken. When one of legal size is caught, its vise-like claws are secured with strong rubber bands, and it is unceremoniously thrown into a holding crate. "Shorts" (undersized lobsters), "eggers" (females carrying eggs), oversized lobsters (carapaces longer than five inches), and females identified by notches in their tails, must, by law, be thrown back. In Maine's inshore fishery, it is rare for someone to repeatedly flout the law, since to do so not only invites large fines, but is also counterproductive.

As each trap is emptied, Paul Lord takes over from his son, replacing the empty bait bag with a fresh one, closing the lid, and hurling the trap back into the sea. The entire operation takes but a few minutes against the angry whine of the HydroSlave—the pot hauler—and the steady growl of the idling boat engine. A canopy of seagulls adds to the din, the airborne scavengers hoping for any discards of fish or bait.

If the noise doesn't assault one's senses, the smell will. Lobster bait is a pungent, slimy amalgam of ripening fish and guts tied into individual bait bags, one for each trap. On a pitching sea, the combination of rotting fish and diesel fumes can be a heady, nauseating mix punctuated only occasionally by a random whiff of blessedly fresh salt sea air.

The routine goes on nearly all year, save for the worst months in winter. Depending on the season, as well as on the abundance and price of lobster, fishermen may choose instead to go crabbing or to harvest sea urchins—a delicacy

to Asian palates, prized for the slippery roe that rests inside a tiny round shell bristling with spikes. Out of season, however, the urchins are merely a nuisance; they clutter up lobster pots and are derisively dismissed as "whore's eggs" as they are hurled overboard.

Scallops and mussels are other important sea crops down east, though their means of harvest—towing a dredge on the ocean floor—worries conservationists and angers lobstermen. Anyone who drags on the bottom inevitably runs the risk of cutting the lines to lobster traps, even if their location is clearly marked by buoys bobbing on the water's surface. Angry words are often traded when a lobsterboat and dragger come near each other, and more than once such a confrontation has escalated into gunfire, requiring the state to set fishing boundaries.

Today, however, there is no talk of confrontation, only the pleasant monotony of hauling traps, interrupted every so often by sips of hot black tea to take the chill out of the early morning air. Just once, another lobsterboat, the *Miss Priss,* pulls near, and David and his father exchange brief greetings with the captain, noting with satisfaction that his catch this day is as meager as theirs.

As Paul muscles each baited and weighted trap back into the sea, yards of pot warp fly after it, perilously close to him. This is a dangerous time, when fast-disappearing line can entangle an unwary fisherman's leg and hurl him over the side, to follow the heavy, plunging trap to the bottom. At the stern of the Lords' boat, in a makeshift sheath bolted to the side, is a razor-sharp knife—a fisherman's one last chance, if he is lucky enough to catch himself at the rail.

One can only wonder about the tragedy aboard the *Joanie Lynne* and the death of Milton Anthony. But the physical evidence was tragically plain. "That Anthony had been pulled overboard was evident from the scuff marks on his boat and the absence of the gaff he used to snare his trap lines," the *Downeast Coastal Press* reported. "Where it happened was determined by local fishermen, who hauled his traps and noted the spot where one was freshly baited and the next was not."

Anthony had been fishing alone.

Jonathan Kinney, the Coast Guard Chief who ordered the sea and air search for Anthony's body, noted that this was the second drowning he had investigated in less than a year.

"I hate to see these guys go without a sternman," he said.

In 1998 a human shinbone brought to the surface by a scallop dragger the previous winter was identified by DNA testing as that of Milton Anthony. Divers could recover no other remains. The bone was laid to rest in a specially built coffin two years to the day after Anthony disappeared.

ICE-CREAM STAND

New England boasts the nation's highest per-capita consumption of ice cream. Any explanation of this phenomenon, especially in Maine, must credit two items: maple syrup and Grape-Nuts cereal.

Who can resist the ambrosial, cholesterol-laden combination of local maple syrup, walnuts, heavy cream, and sugar? Certainly maple walnut is popular elsewhere, but in Maine, where the maple syrup is the real thing—not some scientist's chemical-substitute fantasy—this ice cream is the stuff of legend.

But Grape-Nuts?

It takes a while for the uninitiated to appreciate the qualities of the Grape-Nuts ice cream made by Gifford's, a family-owned Maine dairy. After all, Grape-Nuts cereal eaten by itself can break a tooth. But mixed in with Gifford's rich vanilla ice cream, the slightly softened breakfast staple becomes a chewy counterpoint to the creamy vanilla and can make one forget forever the *arriviste* appeal of Chunky Monkey or Rocky Road.

R E U N I O N

The large, warm kitchen of Mick and Gloria Christie's home in Lubec was a gathering place of sorts—for friends and neighbors, as well as for tourists. Visitors continually trooped through the no-frills bed-and-breakfast, made luxurious by the cakes, breads, pies, preserves, homegrown vegetables, and gourmet meals that these two Maine natives provided with good humor and grace. That was the drill for the warmer times. After first frost, when the evergreens are ready for harvest, Mick and Gloria spent hours tipping in their woods so that Gloria could make the lush holiday wreaths she hung from the side of the barn for all to see, admire, and, of course, buy.

The Sunday morning of this portrait, the kitchen was unusually quiet—no customers dropping in for a loaf of freshly made anadama bread or a quart of strawberry preserves—so the picture-taking went on without delay. As the last of the equipment was being packed, however, a car pulled up. Two women got out and made their way to the side door that led past a rack of checked flannel shirts and into the kitchen.

As the visitors entered, Gloria let out a scream, then raced to hug the handsome woman whose gray hair mim-

icked hers. It was Gloria's sister, whom she hadn't seen in fourteen years.

Oh, they had spoken often enough on the phone, but—as is typical of small towns—there never seemed to be a right time to get in the car and visit. Until today.

Mick Christie died less than a year after these photographs were taken.

Town Meeting

Democracy is not pretty. Giving everyone his or her say takes time and can try the patience. Ask George McGovern. In 1972, the Democratic National Convention that nominated him for president was so rent by controversy, so dominated by supplicants, celebrants, and complainers—all using their fifteen minutes of fame from the podium and the convention floor—that McGovern didn't give his acceptance speech until three in the morning, to a television audience of insomniacs.

Maine town meetings can be like that. Only instead of being nationally televised, their reach extends only as far as local-access cable.

The tradition is as old as the republic: allowing voting members of a community the right to stand and be heard. However, something notable sets a New England town meeting apart from, say, a city council hearing at which public witnesses are heard, or a school board meeting at which questions are taken from the floor. Here, when the question finally is moved, everyone—not just members of the city council or members of the school board or members of the planning commission—casts a vote.

Everyone.

It is a right and a responsibility that many, if not most, Mainers take seriously every year when the warrant for the town meeting is approved by the local board of selectmen, and the date for the annual meeting is agreed on. In fact, one might argue that larger-than-average turnouts by Maine voters in state and national elections are a direct result of the get-involved tradition of the town meeting.

For example, in 1996, Maine voted in high, if not record, numbers in the presidential election, even as the rest of the country set new marks for low turnout. Important statewide ballot issues doubtless spurred the '96 numbers, but the fact remains that, for whatever reasons, Maine voters exercised their franchise in greater numbers than did voters elsewhere.

Town meeting debates rarely involve cosmic issues. Rather, the town warrant—actually a laundry list that is made available to voters days before the meeting—tends to cover such bread-and-butter matters as whether to resurface a road or increase the school budget or expand the meager police force from two officers to three. But that doesn't mean feelings can't run high. Once, for example, during a sweltering summertime town meeting in rural Mattawamkeag, residents fed up with their tax bills voted to simply eliminate the police and public works departments. Then, according to the *Bangor Daily News,* "as people swatted bugs and fanned themselves to keep cool, the tension rose. . . . By 11:30 P.M., the heat and stress of the meeting caused first-time moderator Vernon Robichaud, 72, to faint."

Robichaud was revived and sent home. His replacement, Dean Libby, soldiered on until after one the next morning, when the meeting finally adjourned.

"This used to be a good town," declares selectman

Cressa Garland, who resigned after the rancorous meeting. "People used to care about one another. Now all they want to do is cut each other's throats."

But Mattawamkeag, happily, is an exception. Raucous though a town meeting may get, it rarely degenerates into anarchy.

Take what happened a year later, in another small Maine town.

A few weeks before town meeting, one of the town's selectmen was arrested after getting into a drunken brawl with her sister and her sister's boyfriend. The woman reportedly was upset with her sister's lifestyle—to the point of ripping a phone off the wall and kicking sister and boyfriend out of the house. At the town meeting a few weeks later, one might have expected something to be

said—at least in passing—during the evening's lengthy debate on various issues, some of them contentious, as the selectman let her views be known.

But there was no comment at all. And when she spoke forcefully and effectively on various town issues, her neighbors listened. (That fall, she was reelected easily to the board of selectmen.)

It was as if a favorite uncle had downed one too many scotches at Thanksgiving dinner and then made an embarrassing scene. But in the morning he was sober—and he was still everyone's uncle. So, too, was the selectman given the benefit of the doubt that evening, as she and her fellow citizens went about the mundane but important business of running their town.

EVERGREEN

A native Mainer once asked a friend who had a summer place a few miles up the road for permission to visit the friend's property after first frost and harvest tips from the evergreens there for Christmas wreath-making.

"Sure, Mick, help yourself," the friend said.

"Well, could you give me a piece of paper that says I can do it?" the Mainer asked.

"Do you really need one?"

"Are you kiddin'? You can get shot for tippin' on somebody's land without permission."

Down east, the extra income from tipping (removing the ends of boughs from Douglas fir, spruce, and other conifers) can mean the difference between making it comfortably through the end of the year or staring a cold, hungry winter in the face. Tipping and home wreath-making are a way of life here, and those with large numbers of evergreens on their property don't take kindly to tip rustling. "No Tipping" signs dot some areas of the Maine woods as often as "No Trespassing" and "No Hunting" signs.

Because of the abundance of raw material and the comparative ease of production, this is one of Maine's (and America's) last cottage industries. In the weeks after the first frost, the evergreen tips "set" and grow dormant, preserving their color and fragrance. Local people—mostly women and children but many men as well—then begin a feverish marathon of wreath production, often setting up on the kitchen table or in a special place in the barn.

They sell to local merchants or wholesalers, who then offer the wreaths all over the country, especially in the South where evergreens are scarce to nonexistent. Other locals simply gather tips and sell them directly to wreath makers, at rates that rarely exceed twenty-five cents a pound. But, in sufficient numbers of pounds, that can translate into real money—well over a thousand dollars in some cases. In the poorer communities of Washington and Hancock counties, it is not unusual for whole families, many of whose members were raking blueberries or digging clams months earlier, to earn extra "tippin' money" in late October and early November.

Every year a tipper's worst fear (besides a dry spring that will mean less abundant brush) is a late frost, because that translates into a shorter time in which to gather the tips and sell them before the holidays. Inevitably, some will cut corners. One local wreath maker recalls a year when it was obvious that some of the people he bought from had tipped before the first frost in order to have more to sell. "We had some wreaths starting to turn brown even before we shipped them," the wreath maker grouses. "It's a good source of income," he concedes, "so sometimes the ethics slide."

So good an income source, in fact, that a rare few have turned wreath-making into an industry.

Doug Kell's footloose father began Kelco Industries in the early seventies, when he tired of renting rowboats to tourists and selling Christmas trees from a truck. Today this wreath, garland, and tree business, which Doug runs along with other family members, sells about fifty thousand wreaths

a year from its plant in Milbridge. But that pales in comparison to the three *million* wire wreath frames that the company ships to home wreath makers every season. In fact, the Kelco mail-order catalog is as much a place to find production equipment as it is a source of fragrant things to decorate the front door and hearth. There are wire frames, mechanical garland makers, and bow-making machines, not to mention miles of ribbon, faux holly and blueberries, and thousands of pine cones, each fitted with a serrated plastic end for easy insertion.

"We're probably the number one supplier to the people in the Christmas tree business and the wreath-producing and retailing business," Kell says in mid-November as he moves through a small but bustling complex of shacks and Quonset huts in the heart of town. In one building, heated by a blazing wood-burning stove, some two dozen women work intently at machines that turn thousands of tips into yard upon yard of fragrant garland. (The smell of the evergreens in the heated building is overwhelming, discernible even from outside.)

Kell says his father was a "jack-of-all-trades" who grew up on a farm in Brielle, New Jersey, and who ran sport-fishing boats in Maine during the summer in the mid-'50s. One year, he decided to buy three truckloads of Christmas trees and bring them home to New Jersey. Those evergreens all but flew off the trucks, Doug says, and "the business kind of grew from there." Finally, in the '70s, the senior Kell

decided to follow his heart and his pocketbook to Maine full-time. Thus, Kelco Industries was born.

Today, the operation is nothing at all like the cottage wreath-making industry that spawned it. But to think of Kelco as an evergreen Microsoft would be wrong since at peak season the company employs perhaps 120 to 130 people, up from a year-round staff roughly half that size. By down east standards it is a large business, yet the feel of the place is decidedly small town, especially in the tiny retail outlet that is tacked onto the company's offices, facing coastal Route 1. Here, on this November day, several women of different ages, all bundled hard against the oncoming cold, chat amiably, placing orders for more wire frames, more ribbon. One can't help but feel that this plain wood-paneled room is more meeting place than store, needing only a potbellied stove to set the scene decades back in time.

Before returning to his work, Doug Kell notes that his family owns a 400-acre evergreen farm. In addition to supplying Christmas trees for the retail market, Kelco can now do its own tipping, as well. This is a more efficient way of doing things, surely, but it offers another advantage: Doug and his father don't have to worry that they'll be ready to ship thousands of wreaths, only to discover that some of their brush has come from folks who, facing a late frost and an empty wallet, jumped the season and tipped too soon.

OUTFITTER

He looks like a young Ernest Hemingway and, in fact, has written and photographed a book about northern Maine. But Martin Brown has made his reputation as one of the best expedition outfitters in the state, leading not only canoe but seaplane expeditions all over Maine, Canada, and beyond.

His rustic headquarters and home fronts hard on Cathance Lake, north of Machias, and he notes that a structure like this one could not be built so close to the water today. Save for the bright colors of the fiberglass canoes that are stacked neatly in the compound, Sunrise County Canoe Expeditions might be a throwback to the '30s and '40s, so weathered and so obviously authentic are the surroundings.

In fact, as Brown gazes out the window of his home, his hand resting on a huge backpack that he used on a just-ended adventure, one can't help thinking that a set designer happening upon this place would buy it all, down to the weathered maps on the wall. It would be the perfect hedge against the day when a commercial photographer or movie director would need to create the identical look on a Hollywood set or in a New York studio.

W E E P I N G   M A D O N N A

The day the weeping Madonna arrived in Brewer, the heavens opened and the skies darkened with thunder and fury.

The International Pilgrim Virgin Statue of Our Lady of the Rosary of Fatima is a thirty-three-pound, four-foot-high wooden image of the Virgin Mary that has traveled the world. It has been escorted since 1975 by Louis Kaczmarek, a sixty-two-year-old native of Flint, Michigan, who says he has seen the statue weep on two occasions. He has made it his life's work to preach obedience to Mary and "the wonders she performs," on behalf of the World Apostate of Fatima.

So it is that on this stormy, late-summer day Kaczmarek and the statue come to St. Joseph's Roman Catholic Church in Brewer to take part in an afternoon mass of thanksgiving and rededication. The faithful stream into the modern, high-vaulted church long before the five o'clock service, to kneel before the tiny statue that sits at one end of the white-draped altar. Some whisper the decades of the rosary; some take pictures of the statue's benign—and dry—face. At its base is a small sign.

"Please—Do Not Touch Her," the words read, "She Will Touch You."

The original "Pilgrim Statue" (the Madonna in Brewer this day is said to be an equally miraculous replacement) was made by a Portuguese sculptor, José Thedim. He was present near Fatima in Portugal in 1917 when witnesses said the Virgin Mary appeared several times to warn of an even greater world war than the one raging at that time "if men do not cease offending God." Thedim's statue, which is also purported to have wept, is still in Portugal.

Virtually all who kneel before this "traveling Madonna" tonight are from Brewer, nearby Bangor, or one of the other small towns that hug the Penobscot River. The crowd is young and old, male and female, and the worshippers wear everything from jogging clothes to Sunday best. But one man is different. His bulky frame sports a rumpled striped shirt and dark chino pants. He does not kneel in the pews with the others to offer up his prayers. Rather, he makes it a point to say his rosary alone, kneeling on the floor, with only a boat cushion for comfort. He gives his name as Frank and says he has followed the statue all over the country. When asked how he can afford this, he mentions a disability pension. He also says that he is writing a book.

What about?

"About God," Frank replies.

The storm continues to rage as the mass begins, celebrated by Monsignor Joseph Harvey, a tall avuncular man with a deep voice and soft manner. As the traditional welcome to the faithful begins, the lights in the church suddenly go out, plunging the hall into semi-darkness. Additional candles are lit at the altar and the mass proceeds, amid a warm glow and jokes from the celebrant that Mary is sending a message. Within minutes, however, the lights came back on.

Even to a non-practicing Catholic, the unchanging rhythms and familiar formulas of the mass evoke the

comforting memories of childhood: incense and devotion, whispered prayers, lighted candles, and simple faith. It feels good to be back, even as a spectator.

"We do not worship the statue of Mary," declares Kaczmarek, an intense, balding man with small eyes and a smooth delivery. He has been invited to deliver the Homily to the capacity crowd. "That would be the sin of idolatry. Throughout her history, the Catholic Church has consistently and adamantly forbidden the worship of images. Catholics pray to Mary, to the angels, and to the saints. They worship God alone."

In his book describing his own personal pilgrimage with the statue, Kaczmarek writes that he has actually seen the Madonna weep twice: once in 1980 in Carthage, New York, and two years earlier in Las Vegas, Nevada. On this latter occasion, Kaczmarek notes, the statue wept for three days during heavily attended services at a local church. The suspected reason: "the legalization of prostitution in a number of Nevada counties."

To those who scoff at these stories, Kaczmarek simply quotes Franz Werfel, who wrote "The Song of Bernadette":

"For those who believe, no explanation is necessary; for those who do not, no explanation is possible."

The skies are unrelenting as the sung mass ends to the stirring, almost martial strains of "Holy God, We Praise Thy Name," that venerable rouser familiar to any veteran of parochial schools. With the last strains of the exultant hymn still ringing, the hundreds of congregants scamper for their cars, a few staying behind to chat with Kaczmarek, who stands at the back of the church to greet well-wishers and occasionally to sell and sign his book. Within minutes, though, the church is back to normal.

An evening nuptial mass is scheduled to follow immediately, and as Kaczmarek puts away his books and hands out the last of his scapulars, the bride, an umbrella held over her head by her mother, breezes into the church. She is oblivious to all but what is to come, and goes downstairs to a holding room to make ready for her wedding.

L I V I N G   C A N V A S

James O'Neil's egg tempera studies of his down east environment call to mind the best of America's landscape painters. Outside the state, gallery sales attest that the appeal of his work reaches beyond Maine's borders. And the frenzy in his north Lubec studio whenever a new exhibition looms is evidence that virtually all of his inventory is sold as soon as it hits the wall, leaving hardly anything for the next show.

There is little of the temperamental artist about this bearded and friendly young man. He has a boyish, high-pitched laugh that punctuates his soft voice and, when not painting, he is making music, often in local bands and at nearby gatherings.

He is skilled both with tools and paintbrush. Jim built his home and his studio, and he is especially fond of the latter, which boasts a two-story, north-facing wall of glass. It lets him work all day by natural light, a luxury that artists in more "civilized" urban settings often can only dream of.

MAKING MUSIC

It started with a fishing trip and ended with five used pianos and egg-crate-covered walls. Bruce Potterton, a concert-trained pianist and music teacher from New York, followed what once seemed like a dream and now runs what may be the only piano workshop of its kind in Maine, if not the entire country.

Potterton's SummerKeys total immersion piano workshops—and the free classical music concerts he sponsors (and often performs in) for his adoptive town of Lubec—are a resounding success. And, they reflect one way that small communities in Maine fill their cultural needs against the twin constraints of limited cash and poor accessibility. Places like Lubec, Machias, Eastport, and Cutler—all as isolated as they are beautiful—are so far from commercial entertainment that going out, even to a movie, becomes a major production. From here, for example, the nearest movie theater is in Milbridge, more than an hour away.

So people often improvise, relying on local talent in community theater and music groups. They also "import" performers who can be drawn from more populous and profitable venues to the south on the promise of a nominal fee augmented by the lure of some of the most beautiful scenery imaginable.

The practice is neither new nor limited to this part of the country. In some ways it calls to mind traveling bands of players and minstrels. Closer to home, one can imagine the men and woman who perform in church basements and at baked-bean suppers enjoying a wider audience after previously having played only for a few friends and family around the woodstove in winter.

And who during the summer would deny a professional musician on vacation the pleasure of playing for his or her supper to an appreciative audience in a glorious setting?

When Bruce Potterton first came to Maine in 1990, it was to go fishing with a friend. He didn't know it at the time, but the trip would tie him to Maine forever.

"I'm a real-estate buff," recalls Potterton, a diminutive man with an open, friendly face. "Wherever I go, I love to look at properties. I can never afford them, but I like to look and say, 'Wouldn't it be nice . . .'

"We got as far as Machias. We were going up the main street and I was seeing these crazy prices being advertised." The "crazy prices" were for homes in Lubec, at the easternmost edge of Washington County. "I took a look at the town and I thought, 'My God, this is beautiful'. . . . I came home and I couldn't get the place out of my mind."

Within a year, Potterton had found a white clapboard house that overlooked Johnson's Bay. The oil burner and electrical system were new, half the roof was new, the view was spectacular, and the price was right. He bought it.

Eventually, Potterton's love of teaching music meshed with his love of down east Maine. SummerKeys, a piano workshop, was born.

He bought five used pianos and placed them throughout the house, making ready for a weekly complement of students who would experience an intense five-day regimen of learning, practice, discussion, and performing. But how was Potterton to muffle the sound of five people practicing simultaneously under the same roof yet not go broke on expensive soundproofing?

The egg crates were an inspiration. They worked like a charm, even giving each practice room the look of a recording studio—or, it must be said, a padded cell.

There is a wonderful commonality in listening to musicians perform in less buttoned-up circumstances. Take the Machias Bay Chamber Concerts. During the summer, they are held weekly at the Congregational Church in Machias and feature both local musicians and world-class talent from away. Regardless of who is performing, the evening's program always ends with cookies and lemonade in the church basement. Some visiting musicians, like renowned cellist Leslie Parnas, have been playing in Machias for so many years that they are greeted over refreshments like visiting relatives rather than classical musicians from New York or Boston.

The local talent includes Greg Biss, a gifted classical pianist who makes his living both as a piano tuner and a commercial diver. There's also Gene Nichols, who teaches and plays many instruments, but who prefers to limit his Bay Chamber involvement to writing richly detailed program notes for each concert and acting as page-turner for visiting musicians. (He's been doing this for so long that he gets his own applause when he walks onstage.)

For years, the Machias Bay Chamber Concerts were virtually the only source of live classical music in the area.

Then, happily, a bequest from Bruce Potterton's late mother allowed him to begin his own series of musicales in Lubec: the Mary Potterton Memorial Piano Concerts. Held in the local Catholic Church hall, these free concerts showcase the teachers and musicians that Potterton brings to Maine for his students. Like the Bay Chamber Concerts, these performances (always scheduled so they don't conflict with the events in Machias) have the look and feel of a recital in a friend's parlor.

And, as in Machias, there are always cookies and lemonade afterward, the refreshments strategically located near a donation basket for the piano-tuning fund.

Finally, a season rarely goes by without local bands making appearances in towns up and down the coast. The Orange River Band, the Black Socks Band, Crossing the Borders, and—at one time—the rock group Down East Troop-A-Dors, make music for small audiences, be it at weddings, fairs or fund-raisers, or low-price concerts. The repertoire ranges from Dixieland to classical, from folk to rock: literally something for everyone. Jim O'Neil of Lubec, who has played in several of these bands, is actually a nationally known artist, but he is as adept on guitar, bagpipes, and fiddle as he is with brush and egg tempera. He is also a woodworker and has fashioned several of the instruments he plays, including a triangular-based stringed affair that he says is a cross between a guitar and a bazouki. He calls it a gadzookie.

DAY'S END

It is a measure of the grace with which Mainers greet visitors that Damon and Janis Lesbines pose for their portrait within minutes after Damon returns home from fourteen hours of lobstering.

The Lesbines' home, in Columbia, tells volumes. It was originally a simple cabin with no electricity or running water, but the couple painstakingly turned it into a haven, adding a porch here, a second story there. There is running water now, but the necessary room is still an outhouse, and the living room, with its beautiful ceiling of dried flowers from the garden, is lit by a pair of forty-watt bulbs.

CROSSING THE BRIDGE

On yet another spectacular summer day down east (though, in truth, yesterday was wretched), the United States and Canada are reaffirming their friendship on a windswept bridge over the Lubec Channel. The ceremony stretches into two countries and two time zones, but it is as intimate as it is international.

There's Ed Muskie, former governor of Maine, U.S. Senator and U.S. Secretary of State, standing by the new Canadian customs shed on Campobello Island, New Brunswick. Dressed in a blue blazer and cotton slacks, a tartan cap perched lightly on his head, he talks casually with the handful of people, American and Canadian, who are here to mark the thirtieth anniversary of the bridge linking Lubec and Campobello.

This structure, now called Roosevelt Memorial Bridge in honor of FDR's summertime retreat on the Canadian island, is taken for granted by most tourists and locals alike. It is an international gateway, and one must go through customs at either end. The scrutiny, however, is often so perfunctory, the attitude so friendly ("U.S. citizens? Bring anything back from Canada?") that one barely takes a foot off the gas pedal when heading back into Maine.

The ties between the residents of Lubec and Campobello are so strong as to make their differences seem invisible. It once was common practice for Canadian mothers to bear their children on the American side of the bridge to give them the benefit of dual citizenship. Canadian currency is so common in Lubec that you often get it in change. (It is highly discounted, though, when offered in payment on the U.S. side.) In June, the local Maine paper, the monthly Lubec Light, runs the photos of the graduates of Campobello High School next to those of Lubec High.

Until construction of the bridge, crossing the water between Lubec and Campobello was an adventure befitting the rum running and other illegal activities so common in the area's past. Local historian Frank P. Noyes notes, "what organization [for traversing] there was existed primarily to expedite the smuggling trade, which had been a cornerstone of the local economy." The automobile finally prompted some to seek ways to improve things, and there were various attempts to establish a more formal vehicle ferry. Franklin Roosevelt, Jr., recalled one of these ferries, "which was pushed alongside by a fishing boat, and you drove on in the old days on the Lubec side of the beach, and you drove off on the other side. . . . It was quite a hairy crossing when the tide was running."

FDR himself is believed to have supported the concept of a bridge to his "beloved island," reportedly even discussing it during World War II with then-Canadian Prime Minister McKenzie King. But his sons recalled more reluctance. James Roosevelt said he was "not sure how enthusiastic [father] was [about a bridge] because . . . he liked the island to be rather rustic and not too invaded by too many people." After all, the Roosevelt compound never had electricity.

Financed jointly by the United States and Canada, the bridge was finally completed in 1962—seventeen years after FDR's death. Not long afterward, the two nations created a visitor's center (in the world's first international park) for the benefit of the thousands who flock each summer to the lovingly preserved Roosevelt home.

So it is that on this day—August 2, 1992—the bridge giving access to the president's retreat and its island is being rededicated.

To a journalist used to covering Washington, D.C., the scene is charmingly informal: no elbowing TV crews or shouting reporters, no officious staff people or strong-arm security types. There are just a few officials going over the drill among themselves, and the few local press people who show up are content to leave them alone.

At noon, as a gentle wind blows off the Lubec Narrows, two runners in T-shirts and shorts—one male, one female— start from either end of the bridge and jog the approximately 435 feet to the bridge's midpoint, carrying their respective country's flag and a roll of red crepe ribbon that unfurls in the breeze. At mid-bridge Muskie and his counterpart for the occasion, Canadian Member of Parliament Greg Thompson, tie the ribbons together, then undo them in a symbolic reopening.

Muskie, who was a vigorous seventy-eight then, was a member of the Roosevelt Park Commission and an international lawyer. A politician accustomed to the important bustle of public business, he maintained offices in Washington, D.C.; Maine; Moscow, capitol of the then Soviet Union; and elsewhere until his death in 1996 at age eighty-two. But it says something about the pull of this place that he

eagerly took part in a ceremony that drew but a hundred people at most to a windswept bridge and later to an unused lighthouse on Campobello's Mulholland Point.

There was no podium for the ceremonies on the point; the crowd was so small, everyone could see. There were no microphones either; unamplified voices carried perfectly well in the clean salt air. Christopher Roosevelt, FDR's grandson, was representing the family. He said he would never forget his first visit to Campobello, in 1967, because that happened to be when the Queen Mother, traveling on the Royal yacht *Britannia,* stopped off to see the Roosevelt home. Platooned into being the Queen Mother's guide, Christopher offered his arm, then quickly confessed to her highness that he knew as little about the compound's rooms as she did.

As they entered his grandfather's home, Roosevelt recalled, the Queen Mother "put her other hand on my arm and said, 'Isn't it wonderful, we will be discovering this place together.'"

On this day in 1992, every speaker talked, of course, of the special ties that have created the world's longest undefended border and how, in this case anyway, good bridges make good neighbors.

After perhaps an hour, the ceremonies were over. There was a final blessing and a smattering of applause. Then the event ended as informally as it had begun, as if two friends had passed each other on the street, waved hello, then went on about their business.

WHALE-WATCHER

"When I was a kid, you'd see ten or twelve whales now where you're seein' one—they're here to feed on the herrin', don't you know."

Grayson Mitchell, a burly man with a weathered face from years on the water, speaks in the musical singsong of New Brunswick, Canada, as he stands on the mossy hilltop at East Quoddy Head, surveying the magical sunset that plays out on the water hundreds of feet below him. In the distance, regularly shooting water from their blowholes, a handful of whales cavorts in the fish-rich waters, oblivious to the binoculars and telescopes of the people who stand on the hilltop to enjoy the evening's show.

It is one of the most spectacular sunsets, in one of the most spectacular settings. You get to it by leaving Maine and driving seven miles across Campobello Island—racing the sun if you time it right—and parking just a few yards from the crest of the hill that affords a panoramic view of Head Harbour as well as East Quoddy Light. The lighthouse is stark, beautiful, and candy-striped—like its counterpart in Lubec, just a few miles to the west.

Unlike the U.S. lighthouse, which sits at the edge of Quoddy Head National Park, the East Quoddy light occupies its own rocky promontory, seemingly isolated from the rest of Campobello. In this place of prodigious tides, it is possible at low water to climb down a narrow steel ladder to the bay floor and walk the hundred or so yards to another ladder that leads up to the lighthouse.

But you visit the light on foot at your peril. A big white sign on the mainland point warns that the incoming tide is slow but inevitable. More than once someone has been stranded there, enthralled by the lighthouse view, his escape blocked by the incoming and dangerously cold Fundy tide. But what comes in also goes out, and the marooned visitor would be able to walk safely back to the mainland—going down one ladder and up the other—after a mere eight hours.

In the waning light, Grayson Mitchell swats at a mosquito and speaks of the distant whales as if they were huge companions, even friends.

"The only time they act up," he says, "is when they're feedin'. We'd be out there on the water, and they'd be fishin' for the same thing we were. Once in a while one'd nudge the boat. They can be as gentle as if I reached over and touched you.

"But a seventy-five-foot whale can make you take notice when you're in a twelve-foot dinghy."

MOTHER NATURE

She rowed virtually until the day she died. Ruth Farris was a fixture in the tiny coastal town of Cutler, and her rugged, weathered face reflected generations of self-sufficient Maine women who, with their husbands, carved out a rewarding, though never easy life from the water, farms, and fields down east. Her father was keeper of the lighthouse on Little River Island near Cutler, and Ruth spent the better part of her childhood living on the island, loving the water and feeling most comfortable when riding upon it.

"I row every day," she told the *Downeast Coastal Press* in 1993. "I don't want any outboard motor. I want the rhythm of that oar dipping in the water."

Island living suits only those who seek it out. Ruth's parents were living on Monhegan Island when she was born in 1920, and she recalled the special hardships that have to be endured for the pleasure of living in splendid and beautiful isolation.

"One time we had a cow that fell off the island and broke her neck. . . . She'd fallen off the highest side of the island. I remember, though, we had to get down there and get her bell."

Ruth would play with her brothers, the three children pretending they were lobster fishing. "We'd play with miniature boats in the puddles," she remembered. "We'd catch these bugs and put them in the 'lobster car'. . . . It was a wonderful childhood."

When she grew up, Ruth married Glenn Farris, and together in Cutler they raised their two daughters, Delia and Celia, both now in their fifties. The family lived a simple life of hard work and play that earned Ruth the nickname Mother Nature for her love of the outdoors. "I'm always picking up things to keep the town clean," she explained. "I've made paths, studied birds, done a lot of woodcarving."

She also was a regular at the local grange and at her church. For more than fifty years, she chaired the Cutler Methodist Church suppers and Fourth of July dinners.

But those in Cutler will probably remember her most fondly as the spry old lady who loved to row her boat, the woman whose very act of being on the water, alone and independent, personified what it means to be from Maine.

BLESSING OF THE FLEET

Every summer, the small towns up and down the Maine coast turn out for the traditional blessing of the local fishing fleet. It's usually a day for a little music, some outdoor food, and a pleasant time in the sun. On this day in Lubec, the participants include residents of the local nursing home, who have front-row seats for the passing parade of boats.

THE LAST SMOKEHOUSE

A century ago, when clipper ships plied the coast of Maine and graced the harbor of almost every port that could take them, there were sixty-nine sardine canneries throughout the state. The shiny little fish—small herring, actually—were floating silver, and they fueled the economies of many coastal towns, among them Lubec.

Side-by-side with sardine canning went herring smoking, and in the early 1900s John P. McCurdy's grandfather opened his smokehouse in Lubec. For nearly one hundred years, at various locations in the town, McCurdy's processed millions upon millions of fish, brining and smoking the fleshy, oily herring, then shipping them out of state. In the best of times, restaurants and shops in Boston, New York, and other markets paid top dollar for the salty delicacy.

The pungent smell of smoking fish permeated the air in Lubec during the five- to seven-month herring run, just as the red-painted complex of wooden smokehouses and workrooms on Water Street—McCurdy's location for the last several decades—anchored the heart of the tiny coastal town. It was small business, to be sure (John P. employed only twenty-two people in 1990), but it was vital to a local economy hard hit by unemployment. As the last herring smokehouse in the United States, McCurdy's was also a source of pride and accomplishment for those who worked there.

Then, in 1991, the U.S. Food and Drug Administration forced the company to close down—wrongly, as it turns out.

John P. McCurdy himself now stands in the salting house among empty, weathered, wooden tubs, the edges of which have been rubbed round from decades of hard use. A string of bare lightbulbs illuminates a room where once a small ocean of herring would float in water and rock salt for five full days before going through the next step in the ancient ritual.

Standing there in silence with John P., one can imagine the noise and commotion of what turned out to be the final years of McCurdy's Smokehouse, when men like Shirley Fitzsimmons, Doug Hooper, and the late Leeman Wilcox would plunge the long nozzle of the gathering hose into the still-wriggling herring in the belly of a workboat just in from the bay. With a great whoosh, the fish would be sucked up and thrown into the salting room's overhead sluices, then parceled into the wooden holding tanks in a blindingly efficient management of herring traffic.

"This is where we salt 'em," Leeman would tell a visitor over the din, a perpetual cigarette dangling from a mouth that always seemed curled in a shy smile. Walking with a slight stoop, he would muscle each eighty-eight-pound sack of salt chest-high and empty it into a tank, the total number of bags dependent on the level of the fish within. Every other day Leeman would use his spudger, a long wooden-handled tool, to "break 'em up"—agitate the mixture of herring, water, and salt. Then he would add yet another bag of salt "to keep the brine up."

After five days, the herring would be ready to be strung—impaled through the gills—onto hundreds of forty-inch-long wooden poles, dozens of fish packed tightly on each pole. The work would be done quickly, each rubber-aproned man and woman moving with the steady precision of forty,

fifty, or even sixty years' practice, all of it at McCurdy's. Shirley, meanwhile, would ready the fires in the smokehouses.

In each of the dark wooden dirt-floored buildings, he would set alight small mounds of spruce, fir, and, when available, driftwood, then damp them with mounds of sawdust to keep the smoldering going for days at a time. The smoke would rise slowly through the overhead racks, where thousands of salted fish hung on row after row of poles, each pole placed by hand in the great blackened rafters, their position rotated as the days passed. Drop by drop, the fish would shed their oil into the fire, the smoke and smell seeping from the vent windows and spreading all through the town.

The smell of money, people liked to say.

Finally, the fish would be taken to the boning room, where, amid amiable chatter and the fast-moving hands of the women who worked there, each fish would be taken from the stick, beheaded, split in two, gutted, skinned, and packed tightly into a simple box made of wooden shooks, bearing the stenciled legend: "Boned Smoked Herring/Net Wt. When Packed 10 lbs./McCurdy Fish Co./ Lubec, Me."

It was a difficult way to earn a living, but it suited those who did it—for decades at a time—until the end came suddenly in 1991.

John P., as he is known throughout Lubec, is a lean and blunt-spoken man, with a lined face and piercing eyes. Only an occasional broad smile gives him away. He did not go gently into forced retirement and still speaks with anger of the time in 1990 when a federal inspector who had been visiting his plant for years without complaint suddenly announced that McCurdy was in violation of a new federal health regulation. He would have to shut down unless he implemented changes costing more than a quarter-million dollars.

At issue was the way McCurdy operated—the same way his father and grandfather before him had handled fish without one case of food poisoning ever reported: he gutted his catch *after* it was salted and smoked, not before.

"Increases the risk of botulism," the FDA man said, though it later turned out that the new regulation had been based on studies of whitefish, not herring (a key difference since each species reacts differently to the brining and smoking process). To add insult to injury, at least some of the Canadian plants that now have a monopoly on the U.S. herring market clean their fish exactly the same way.

"There was no way I could afford it," McCurdy says with a dismissive, though still pained laugh, as he describes all the new evisceration and refrigeration gear the government wanted him to buy. He pleaded his case in Washington, and then-senator William Cohen managed to buy him enough time to sell off the bulk of his last catch. But that was all. "The way they decided to punish me, you would have thought I'd shot somebody," he told the newspapers at the time.

Barely into his sixties—still years from retirement, by his reckoning—McCurdy figured more fight would be futile and said the hell with it. His options and spirit gone, John P., whose grandfather and namesake had built a once-proud business nearly a century before, shuttered his doors and walked away.

O L D   V E T

The years have slowed his step, and he walks with one of several weathered canes that hang on a rack by the kitchen door. But first impressions of Dr. Joseph A. Thomas of Perry are deceptive.

"Can't talk now, I got an animal on the table!" the eighty-six-year-old veterinarian snapped over the telephone. "I'm here tonight." (Click.)

He doesn't smoke cigars—he chews them. And if Norman Rockwell might not have envisioned a stogie-chomping vet ministering to a puppy needing shots or a rabbit suffering from a tumor, that is real life during Thomas's evening office hours.

You find his office on the road to Perry, but there is no sign. You look instead for the derelict motel a few miles from the turnoff to Eastport. "I bought it because it was a good buy and I could live in it too," he once said. Some years earlier Thomas added the structure that became his office and consulting room, but the place still looks for all the world like the motel that time forgot.

He came down east from the Hudson River Valley in New York, "driven out," he says, by the racial unrest of the turbulent '60s. He blames then-New York Governor Nelson A. Rockefeller for letting rioters run rampant through his town in the name of keeping the peace. So he fled to Maine.

His pale eyes sparkle as he ministers to his animals with a deft and sure hand. This evening Spike, a six-month-old yellow Lab, needs shots and when his owner lifts the fidgety pup onto the examining table, the dog calms immediately under the old vet's gentle touch.

The same can't be said of the rabbit that lies in a fitful torpor following delicate surgery for a large tumor on its neck. "It was a terrible, ugly thing," Thomas says, affronted by the malignant growth. "I had to cut all along the jawbone."

"He stopped breathing on the [operating] table, but we brought him back."

The rabbit, its bloody wound still visible, is covered by a towel as it lies in an old wooden cage. Its owners, a young couple who speak in whispers, stand by the open cage door, alternately petting the prone animal and snapping their fingers in an attempt to get its attention.

"He tried to move his leg," the young man replies.

"That's good, that's good," Thomas says, though he confided to a visitor earlier, before the couple arrived, that he wondered if the weakened rabbit could even survive the anesthetic.

The doctor busies himself as he has for years: with dogs, cats, rabbits, and other small animals. He says he doesn't "do" large animals anymore—too much strain on his heart.

At eighty-six, Thomas has buried virtually all of his friends and relatives. "I'm the only one left," he says with a bare but discernible sadness. He married late in life and lost his wife after nineteen years. They had no children. And if this day has been typical for the old vet, it is sadly atypical as well, for earlier Thomas was forced to check his companion of the last three years into a nursing home. She had developed Alzheimer's, he says, and he was afraid that, if left alone, she might fall and break a hip.

"There's no one here but me," he repeats as he goes about his business, facing loneliness once more, and for the last time.

Dr. Thomas died the following year.

BLUEBERRY HARVEST

In the heat of a down east August, they are in the fields, stooped over close to the ground, wielding heavy, handheld rakes within the white-string boundaries that define their allotted rows.

Secured by pegs in the hard, dry ground, the twine makes each plot straight and narrow, and it doesn't compensate for the boulder or blank spot that will diminish the yield. Still, a raker moves into another's row at his peril. Many, if not most, of the blueberry pickers are local Mainers or Native Americans, though harvest-following migrants round out a workforce that can number in the thousands—spread all over Washington County—before the picking is complete.

It is hard, hot, backbreaking labor, but raking blueberries can mean good money—several hundred dollars a day—for families who can send more than one worker into the sprawling barrens where low-bush blueberries abound.

Hour after hour, harvesters scoop up the fruit with a tool that looks like a dustpan with tines. The rake is heavy and gets heavier by the hour. Ironically, the technology for processing, storing, freezing, and canning blueberries is amazing and rivals any in the food-processing industry. Still, no one has come up with a better way to harvest the precious fruit than by hand, one raker at a time, bent double in the field.

Workers like Maine native Gladys Ganiel are paid a set rate per box—$2.50 to $5, for example, depending on the quality and abundance of the berries. Like Gladys, they bring their boxes to roadside pick-up points, where the fruit is placed in plastic crates. These, in turn, are loaded into trucks for quick transport to the processing plant.

"In Columbia [Maine]," Ganiel writes in a journal that was published in the *Downeast Coastal Press,* "the barrens stretch far and wide—like the Great Plains of the Midwest. Winds can whip across those stark barrens, bristling through the solitary pines or over the scattered rocks."

But other places, like notorious Pork Brook in Beddington, are but "a series of tiny fields surrounded by a forest that seems intent on reclaiming the blueberry land. The forest will stifle all but the most stubborn of winds and bake workers in an unmerciful heat." Still, Ganiel describes the day of which she writes as better than most because "the air is not humid and the breeze possesses some spunk."

Even in mid-August, though, too early a start can be as difficult as one in the hot midday. "The handle of the rake is . . . bone-chilling cold," Ganiel writes, "and the berries feel frozen and sting your hands when you smooth them out to make your boxes level. In the heat of a long afternoon, however, the berries will turn mushy, reminiscent of pie filling. . . ."

Wild, so-called low-bush blueberries are known for their intense flavor and small, almost pellet-like size. They are one of America's few native fruits. Black bears have been know to travel fifteen miles in a day to feast on them, and Native Americans in New England used them not only for

food but for medicine. Blueberries were first canned commercially during the Civil War, when the fruit was shipped south to help feed the Union army.

Like lobsters and herring, wild blueberries are a part of coastal Maine's abundance—poor, small Washington County, for example, is responsible for more than 70 percent of the entire nation's harvest. Unlike waters that can be overfished, blueberry fields with adequate drainage and pollination can produce forever, though they always are subject to the vagaries of drought, downpours, and—the newest threat—pollution. Every summer, the *Ellsworth American* can be counted on to front-page the preharvest estimate of the size of the crop; the paper's banner headline is as reliable as a stock ticker for providing the good news or the bad.

In the fields, though, little thought is given to the big picture; pickers focus only on the small one: how much they will make for the day. A raking crew being given its paychecks is oblivious to everything—a stranger asking directions, for example, or even a boss showing up unexpectedly. Inevitably, tensions can mount—between Anglos and Native Americans, between Latinos and Anglos, between and among every group. A season doesn't pass without a local paper reporting on some assault or mayhem in the blueberry barrens. Real violence, however, is rare since the raking season is short, and there is money to be made.

In Machias, the shire town of Washington County and the place where the annual Blueberry Festival is held every summer, a number of processing plants transform the stoop labor of the many into a true cash crop.

The most sophisticated of these factories is the Maine Wild Blueberry Company, a huge complex that eagerly goes to round-the-clock shifts during harvest season, the better to get the berries processed and to market. Its equipment is state-of-the-art, much of it designed abroad. The key is speed—in stemming and flash-freezing the berries as quickly as possible and in sorting them by grade and size, depending on market and ultimate use. (The Japanese, for example, prefer larger berries and will pay top dollar for them even though there is no difference in taste.)

Of all the operations at the Maine Wild Blueberry Company, the long blue line of the sorting room is the most unusual. There workers—mostly women—sit at long conveyer belts to inspect the berries before they are readied for shipment. Hot though it may be outdoors, the women are bundled against the cold in sweaters and hooded sweatshirts. Every one of the millions of berries they are inspecting is frozen solid, and the room itself is refrigerated.

The work goes on hour after hour, though for a few minutes in every sixty, there is a break. Then the women troop outside the cold room to stand together in a line and touch their hands to their shoulders and stretch their necks in an OSHA-mandated ritual designed to combat repetitive-stress injury.

C A N O E B U I L D E R , S T O R Y T E L L E R

He speaks in low, musical cadences marked by clipped endings and fond memories. His talent for telling stories is as prodigious as his skill at building his version of the Grand Lake Stream Canoe. They're constructed one at a time, all by hand, in the incredibly cluttered workshop that leans at a precarious angle outside his gray-shingled home in Jacksonville, Maine, just east of Machias.

Maurice Berry was eighty-three when he finished his thirteenth "Grand Laker," as these boats are called; he made this one for his son, he explains, "so he could have something that belonged to Pa; something that Pa built.

"This is ash, this is spruce," he tells a visitor, walking the twenty foot, eight-inch length of the great boat. "The ribs and the planking are cedar. The stern board is ash, and the stems are ash. And the deck is—now what did I put in there?—oh, it's ash."

Those who know Berry well call him "Mok," a name that has stuck, if in somewhat different form, for more than three-quarters of a century. It was that long ago when the Indians who lived near Berry's hometown of Chase Mills first saw his head of thick hair and dubbed him "Mop." He is an original, and when he and others like him are gone, there will be a gaping void. Mok Berry has the gift of memory, of times when, as a boy, he would sit wide-eyed, listening to the Civil War stories of old Gus Smith, who had been imprisoned at Andersonville.

He remembers spending barefoot summers working with his father in the Maine woods he so loves. Once, during a freak October snow, his father had to come to school with boots for Mok and his brothers because they had left the house with no shoes at all.

Mok also remembers pining for the salt air of his birth while working at a munitions plant in Ann Arbor, Michigan, during World War II, when his work on the Norden bombsight kept him there for the duration. Was the Midwest air really that different, he is asked. "Oh, I guess so!" retorts Mok. "Sniff that salt water. You can't smell a smell like that in Detroit, I can tell you that. . . ."

Mok was born in Chase Mills on February 25, 1911, in the middle of eleven brothers and sisters. Of these, he is the sole survivor. It was a bitter cold night when Maurice Berry entered the world, and the doctor didn't make it to Cora Berry's side until after Mok had been born. They paid Doc MacDonald anyway: a barrel of flour.

Mok's skill with his hands and his love of making things inevitably brought him to canoe building. For that, he needed a mold on which to construct new hulls. Sensibly, Mok decided to build this form over an old, existing canoe. The original mold, now modified to fit changes he has made in the old Grand Laker design, dominates his workshop. "You know, when you are going into the wind [the traditional Grand Laker] would throw up spray that hit you in the face. So I changed it a couple of ways—in the sheer, some people call it. [The sheer is the upward curve of the gunwale from stern to bow.] You know, waves in the inland lakes are seldom more than sixteen feet apart, no matter how hard the wind blows.

"In fresh water, if you go the right speed, you can hit the top of the next wave from the rear one. I lifted the tumble-away [the angle of the sides relative to the water's surface] from here down to here, and it throws the waves right out parallel to the water."

Mok once had a customer who asked that his new boat be painted a different color on each side. "He was gonna fool the wardens, going up the stream in a red canoe, then back in a green one," explains the veteran builder. "Well, it didn't work very long."

Mok's walk and his work are slower now, but nothing has diminished his wit or his memory. Ask him about the worst time in his life, and he will quickly say it was all those years during the war, away from Maine. "Oh did those lakes stink!" he remembers. "I couldn't wait to get my feet on the ground, away from the concrete, and to smell the ocean again."

His eyes grow distant as he speaks the mantra of a native son: to breathe the air of the piney woods, to walk under a sky of a thousand clouds and a million stars, and to smell the water that "comes from as far away as who knows where."

COUNTRY KITCHEN

Simplicity is still a respected quality in Maine homes. Why, after all, does one need fancy, enclosed cabinets when a few hooks on the wall will do? These well used pots and pans are quite comfortable out in the open in their Lubec kitchen.

C H A I N - S A W   G U Y

There are many ways to artistic fame. Ray Murphy's way is with a chain saw.

Drive east along Route 1 to Ellsworth, and even before you reach him you are aware of a buzz: the angry growl of one of Ray's two dozen chain saws, a set of instruments as precious to him as gold, silver, and platinum flutes are to James Galway.

As precious, but louder.

"Someone else would have to try it, but there's no one ever been successful in doin' it except myself," Ray declares of the chain-saw sculpture that has won him fame throughout the down east region. His work has even earned him a spot in *Ripley's Believe It or Not* (for saw-carving the alphabet on a pencil). "That's kind of a strange thing," Murphy says, "to have something that no one else can do."

A burly man with a full beard and a barrel chest, Ray claims to have invented chain-saw sculpture. In truth, others do it too, but it is easy to credit his claim that no one does it better. Life-size Indians, bears, game fish, birds—as well as his famous pencil—line the walls of the old bus he uses as a traveling museum and a backdrop for his open-air demonstrations. He is proudest of his eagles—also life-size and done with a level of detail that's amazing given that all Ray uses on them is a tree-cutting tool moving at blinding and perilous speed. He did his first eagle more than thirty years ago, on a whim, when he was "just playing around." Ray decided then and there to develop what he felt was a "natural talent."

He never did have any formal art training. "A number of people have told me I should go and learn—that it'd improve my work," he says. "My comment is, why should I learn to do somebody else's work—let 'em copy me!"

Before moving down east, Ray worked all over the west, building log cabins and working in heavy industry. You can't help but notice the missing fingers on one hand, but the injury wasn't the result of the occupational hazard inherent in carving with chain saws; he lost them in a logging mishap.

With a healthy backlog of orders, Murphy enjoys and, frankly, nurtures his renown as an eccentric artist. Once, in the late '70s, Peter Stihl, who invented the chain saw in Germany decades before, visited Ray at his shop, then in the Black Hills of South Dakota. "It was amazing to meet the man that invented the saw," Ray says, but he adds quickly, "He was absolutely amazed to see what I was doing, too."

As Ray speaks, a carload of tourists pulls up, and they watch intently as he wields his saw on a huge block of wood. "I'm working on a lobster," he says with a wide grin. A little girl, no more than ten or eleven, approaches him and asks for his autograph.

"I'll do better'n that!" replies Ray, taking a scrap of wood and securing it to a stump. (One suspects he has done this before.) Revving up his saw, Murphy makes a few quick passes and carves "RAY" into the block. "Here you are, honey," he says, handing the "autograph" to the delighted girl.

"Maybe she'll be a new customer," Ray whispers to a bystander through a sawdust-encrusted smile.

T R I B A L   G A T H E R I N G

Members of the Passamaquoddy Indian tribe, descendants of Maine's first inhabitants, reunite at the Pleasant Point reservation near Eastport to mark this annual gathering with pride and pageantry.

Passing through the reservation to reach the town, one is aware of a mix of housing. There are neatly maintained bungalows; there are poorly kept trailers. Still, anyone who has witnessed the grinding poverty and despair of Indian reservations in the American West would have to concede that, on balance, Pleasant Point lives up to its name.

The festivities this day include dancing and singing, as well as displays of Indian crafts and storytelling. The event begins with a parade that moves through Eastport to Pleasant Point—a promontory surrounded by water—followed by trooping of the colors and singing the national anthem. As always, tourists are fascinated by the dancers—especially those in colorful beads and feathers—and point their long lenses anywhere they can. One onlooker, himself in a loud getup of windowpane plaid pants, gets so close that he appears to be joined at the lens with a man in bright beaded buckskin and a feathered headdress.

DAILY GRIND

Raye's Mustard has been churning out the spicy condiment for decades in Maine's easternmost city, Eastport. It's the only stone-ground mustard mill left in the United States, and though Nancy Raye, who took over the place from her father, offers many different varieties, the recipes all start with bag upon bag of mustard seed that is ground to syrupy perfection in a bath of vinegar and spices.

It is fitting that a place so dependent on old-time granite grinding wheels would look the part down to its power source. Housed in a red wooden factory with mustard-color (surprise!) window frames, the production line comes to life with the growl of a huge engine linked to massive belts of dark harness leather. It is these that turn the grinding wheels round and round in a cacophonous chorus. The result—a river of pungent yellow mustard streaming into big wooden collecting vats—makes one salivate for a sausage.

C O U N T R Y   D O C T O R

ontinuity.

It has been a long time since Dr. Karl Larson took half a pig or a cord of wood in payment for delivering a baby. But back in the '40s, when he was just starting his practice, such compensation was common in a place where cash money was tight and where the more common medium of exchange was the goods derived from saltwater farms and the dense evergreen woods.

Until his recent retirement, "Dr. Karl" still practiced in the coastal town of East Machias, just a few miles from where his late father had been the town's family doctor since 1905. Between them, Old Doc Larson and "young" Dr. Karl contributed nearly a century of doctoring to the families of the farmers, fishermen, and tradespeople of this ruggedly beautiful community.

Working well into his eighties, Dr. Karl kept regular office hours five days a week in a white clapboard building that was built in 1785. His consulting room was from another era—enameled metal cabinets with glass fronts, a weathered oak chair and desk, a well-used examining table— all sitting on a spotless linoleum floor of black-and-white checks. If you had turned on a radio here, you might have

expected to hear news about Bess Truman's engagement or how yet another DiMaggio homer had beaten the Red Sox. Atop one cabinet was a model of a two-masted clipper ship of the type that sailed nearby waters more than a hundred years ago—a gift from a patient.

Dr. Karl made house calls too, mostly on homebound geriatric patients—some younger than he—who couldn't make it to his office or to the hospital miles away in Machias.

Today, Larson's reputation precedes him. Talk to a random handful of people from the area, and the most common response is, "He delivered me." Occasionally, you'll hear, "He delivered me—and my parents." Dr. Karl estimates he has attended the birth of more than one thousand babies. A soft-spoken, reticent man, Larson admits that it is a nice feeling to have brought so many people into the world and to walk among them, as well.

"When you deliver a patient, the parents used to think, 'Well, doctor, you have to take care of him the rest of his life.' It's a closer connection than you have with the rest of your patients."

It is continuity.

SEMI-INVISIBLE MAN

When he taught at the University of Maine in Machias, Professor Herb Martin used to say that minorities in overwhelmingly white Maine suffer from "a lack of exposure . . . an intentional myopia" that makes people of color invisible in the state.

He spent the better part of his years down east trying to correct that in his classes and in the seminars he helped sponsor. There, he would teach students about the rich cultural heritage that exists in Maine, especially among the Native American tribes that still populate the state. A burly bespectacled man, Martin proudly wears the medicine bag that reflects the background and tradition of his Cherokee mother, and he is eloquent in relating the mythical tales of his childhood, learned at his mother's knee. He is determined to pass on these tales, not only to his children but to future generations of all races.

MOTHER'S HELPER

The calf was a beautiful thing—part Jersey, part Charolais. Its long eyelashes shaded large, limpid eyes. The mother cow hovered close by her baby as Carol Prouty—of Lubec, Maine, by way of the British Empire—struggled to keep up with the newborn, which only hours before had found her legs. Exultantly—if unsteadily—the calf scampered across the fenced-in farmyard, never knowing how close it had come to being orphaned. But Carol knew it had been the kindness of her neighbors and of one octogenarian vet that had pulled the mother through—even if the vet had almost succumbed in the process.

Prouty is a relative newcomer to Lubec, only having settled down east in the mid-1980s, after being widowed. A handsome woman in her fifties, Prouty has medium-length blonde hair and well used laugh lines around her eyes and mouth. In her corduroy pants, brown jacket, and mud-spattered boots, she fits well into her surroundings, even if a decade here is only a blink in time in a place where roots go back generations.

Born in England, Prouty lived in Australia, New Zealand, and Newfoundland, but she spent most of her married life in Massachusetts, where her late husband worked in construction and heavy machinery. "I waitressed, bartended, did office work—that's about most of it," she explains in an accent that is equal parts Old and New England. "I really like the climate and being close to the ocean. . . . It's pretty country, it really is, and you have a feeling of freedom. You can breathe. It wouldn't bother me

to walk all around the town of Lubec at midnight. Where my daughter lives in Massachusetts, it's supposed to be a nice place, but you can't walk there. . . . There's muggings and molestings and things like that. It's a shame.

"Oh, you have some crime here and stuff," Carol says, then adds with a laugh, "[but] usually everybody knows who done it and why they done it."

Prouty remembers all too well the near disaster that followed the birth of the lovely calf. "Friday morning, the fifth of November, I could see that the cow was gonna have the calf, so I called Julian Blanch. He came down and checked her and said, 'Well, she won't be too long,'" Carol recalls. "This was about eight in the morning. He came back about ten, and we brought her into the barn. About ten-thirty, the water sac came out and Julian punctured that and pulled the calf out. There was no problem, and everybody was happy, including the mother cow.

"But the next morning when I got up at about six-thirty or seven, the mother was lying flat on the floor in real distress. She was really sick, and I just about flipped—it was very nerve-wracking to see something like that, with so large an animal. So I called Julian and a couple of other neighbors who have animals—Paul Olson and Timmy Scoville. Julian was good friends with Dr. Thomas, and he actually got the old vet to come down.

"Well, poor Doc Thomas got out of his new truck, and he had a heart spell right in this barn. We offered him a cup of tea, but for about fifteen minutes he just sat there in kind of a coma and said 'I'll be all right' at intervals.

"[Finally,] he came out of it and said he was fine, no problem. Thank goodness I had an old armchair in there. He was very old, eighty-five or so, and he couldn't see well and couldn't use his fingers really well. So my neighbors acted on his direction, and we worked on the cow until about seven or eight that night.

"Every time they'd give her medicine, her stomach would blow up, and we'd have to knead it and try to roll her to get the gases out of her belly. We just worked on her like that—there was three men and me. I don't know what I would have done without them. I would have lost the cow.

"They put it down to milk fever, but it could probably have been any internal infection from the birth—like a hoof could have cut her inside and got bacteria, or something like that. They really don't know. Dr. Thomas told me that for one thing, I took too good a care of my cow—she was too fat—and he said the problem is very common in fat cows. Never do they have it in skinny cows."

E L D E R   S T A T E S M A N

Maine is known less for pop celebrities and more for thoughtful luminaries like former senators George Mitchell, Margaret Chase Smith, and Edmund Muskie. Another member of this much-admired fraternity is J. Russell Wiggins, one-time ambassador and publisher of the *Ellsworth American*.

THE SPEECHLESS BROTHERS

For years, the old woman in the nursing home had neither spoken nor smiled. Then the llama came to visit.

Led into the community room, where the old folks had assembled, the animal fixed the woman in its limpid gaze and seemed to communicate in silence, bending its graceful neck to her. Who knows how many years had passed since the woman had stroked a beloved cat or dog, or watched a child approach without apprehension? There was silence in the room.

The woman smiled.

Near his home in Machias, Belden Morse tells this story a few yards from a field that holds half a dozen of these benign creatures. With names like Sea Dawn, Amazing Grace, Sea Breeze, and Felice, the llamas graze languidly, occasionally flicking their six-inch ears in the fading afternoon light. Some of them, new mothers, give suck to their furry babies—beautiful things that wear their thick new coats like goslings.

"They're like a cat," Belden says almost in a whisper. "They'll come up to you when they want to. They're very friendly.

"We started with one male. It was more of a pet thing. We had some sheep, but there was just this fascination with the way the llamas look, the way they hold themselves. I had no intention of gettin' into breedin' and what have you."

Nevertheless, for more than a decade Belden and his wife, Jane Heart, have reared these distant and gentle cousins to the camel. What began with one male grew into a mixed herd of about a dozen, which Belden and Jane raise for breeding. They also harvest the luxurious wool, which rivals that of the llama's other cousins, the vicuna. Llama dung is an excellent fertilizer and can be turned into the soil almost immediately. Other breeders use the placid, sure-footed animals for trekking; they are excellent pack animals, their padded feet gentle to all terrain.

"We know that the ancient Incas and other indigenous peoples of Peru lived with domestic llamas over five thousand years ago," says Jane. In fact, it is believed that feral, or wild, llama herds simply do not exist today. Five thousand years of breeding have produced a strain of animal that, perhaps even more than the dog, is totally comfortable in the presence of humans. Indeed, llamas seem to need the companionship of people like Belden and Jane, whose small farm provides the kind of tranquil environment best suited for these most tranquil of beasts.

"I grew up just down the road from here," says Belden, a solid man with a bushy red beard and a gold-capped front tooth that punctuates his smile. "I'm from a long line of fishermen—my father, his father, and so on. I got into doing construction work [he and Jane are known as The Steeple People for Belden's other specialty: restoring old church steeples], but I always had an interest in animals. We had a small farm—a milk cow, a work horse, a ridin' horse, this sort of thing. But I always wanted to do something that was different, so I think that's why I got away from lobster fishing.

"The llamas have such a personality," says Belden. "They're very intelligent and very quiet. [The Peruvians] call them 'the speechless brothers.' They do make a humming noise, though, and an alarm call if there's a predator in the pasture.

"The sheep drove me nuts," Belden laughs, recalling his childhood. "They were baah-in' constantly. They're sorta stupid. But they know as much as a sheep needs to know, so on that level, they're intelligent. You have to be careful [discussing llamas] around horse people. They'll ask, 'In relationship to intelligence, what are they like in comparison to a horse?'

"Horses can be *real* stupid.

"I can take a young llama and teach him to be halter-trained in four or five sessions. I can teach one to be taken in and out of the van in only three sessions. And I'm only talkin', like, ten-minute sessions. You can't get a horse to climb more than six inches, and the back of that van's a good two feet."

How gentle are llamas? Besides visits to nursing homes, Belden and Jane also bring them to schools and fairs—all as a community service. They invariably find that people are captivated by the llamas' serene demeanor. (Unlike camels, which can be nasty things that would just as soon spit as look at you, llamas tend to spit only at each other and only when they are upset.) You couldn't be bitten by a llama if you tried. Grazers, they have no upper front teeth and chew their cud with upper and lower molars.

The acceptance, if not the outright popularity, of these gentle and useful beasts is certainly growing. A couple of years ago at the Blue Hill Fair, a gardener friend caught up to Belden and Jane, and asked whether she could get some of the llamas' dung to use as fertilizer. Jane replied with a touch of resignation that there was a waiting list for it.

WINTER'S WARMTH

Down-easters are apt to point out that firewood warms you three times: once when you cut it, once when you stack it, and once when you burn it. Heating with wood is still common throughout Maine, and many homeowners pride themselves on neatly organizing the winter's supply of split logs.

R I G G E R S

During the Cold War, Washington insiders joked that one of the prime targets of the Soviet Union during a preemptive nuclear missile strike on the United States would be a hot dog stand.

In fact, the hot dog stand in question was more of a snack bar that happened to sit in the center of the Pentagon's grassy interior courtyard for the lunchtime convenience of employees. Since the Pentagon would obviously be on the Russians' A-list of things to obliterate in time of war, the snack bar at ground zero gave inevitable rise to the joke.

No more bizarre—and just as understandable—is the notion that another key wartime target of the once-mighty Soviet Union would have been the tiny coastal fishing village of Cutler, Maine.

Arguably one of the most bucolic towns in the state, with a protected harbor that is perfect for fishermen and a coastline that is postcard lovely, Cutler's position at the northeastern corner of the country also gives it tremendous strategic importance. It affords a virtually perfect line of radio communication to American ships, planes, and submarines operating in the North Atlantic and Arctic oceans.

To take advantage of this location, the U.S. Navy built the Naval Computer and Telecommunications Station/Cutler. Completed in 1961, the three-thousand-acre complex sits virtually out of sight at the end of the town, yet its most distinguishing feature—twenty-six mammoth radio towers, each one a thousand feet tall—can be seen for miles in any direction.

These very-low-frequency towers can handle two million watts of power, making NCTS/Cutler the most powerful radio station in the world, albeit one with a very small audience for its top-secret transmissions.

The job of maintaining the towers—which means climbing them regularly to ensure proper tension on the miles of wire they support—falls to a rugged group of Mainers, civilians with electrical and mechanical backgrounds. They take a dogged pride in doing a job few others would even consider.

So it was chagrining for these proud riggers to be sent home, if only for a few days, as "non-essential" employees during one of the 1995 federal government shutdowns. Rigger Mike Seeley is philosophical, though. He always feels essential, he says, adding that the people who matter most— his navy bosses—"know that we can get a job done" even when the rest of the government can't function.

S A W Y E R

To the uninitiated, sawmills are huge factories whose hundreds of workers annually turn out millions of board feet of construction-grade lumber for the mass market. In reality, however, the down east region—like the rest of Maine—is dotted with small, one- or two-man operations similar to David Yates's in Lubec. They are more likely to supply local builders with rough-sawn boards for siding or to provide area cabinet-makers with specialty hardwood stock.

TAXIDERMIST

"Of course, fish is about the hardest ones to do because of the colors and all," says Lewis Jones as he shows off a roomful of mounted birds, fish, and other wildlife in his crowded woodshed-turned-workshop in Trescott. "But in the animals, oh, y'know rabbits are quite hard to do because they got such fine skins and they tear very easy.

"They're all pretty much the same in a way, though. 'Course, deer heads—I do more of them than anythin' 'cause that's what I get most call for."

His hand-lettered "Blueberry Ridge Taxidermy" signs dot the highway leading into Trescott and are made to mimic the ones put up by the state to lure tourists to spend their money. He has been at it full- and part-time for nearly twenty years now, but for all the skill attested to by the silent, motionless animals that surround him, he's still not as good at it as he would like to be.

"They'll all give you trouble if you don't study up on them," Jones says as his grandson Seth (then almost four) busies himself among the foxes, rabbits, baby bears, and partridge. "But there's quite a little diff'ence from one species to the other. You never can stop learnin' doin' it. I never can satisfy myself. I don't think any taxidermist can—you're always wantin' to do better, each thing you do, and you see where you can improve as you go along."

In this part of Maine, bears can be so plentiful that at times the younger ones are killed by vehicles. Jones has several such specimens in his shop, brought in by nearby hunters who doubtless didn't anticipate bagging trophies with their trucks.

"That one sittin' down there, I wouldn't say he's much more than a year and a half. That other one, I don't think he's quite a year," says Jones.

Seth, a substantial little boy with round cheeks and dark eyes, isn't much bigger than the bears, which he likes to pet. He volunteers that when he turns four he is going to get a dog, which he plans to name Max.

Rustic though Jones's taxidermy shop may be, he follows the letter of the law and will not mount any game taken out of season, nor sell any migratory waterfowl—either to souvenir seekers from away or perhaps to local armchair hunters. The penalties are just not worth it.

Every one of his transactions, every trophy mounted, goes into the record book that must be submitted to the state capital in Augusta each year. "I can do 'em for a customer if he brings me one, provided they were shot in season," Jones explains. "I can take money for that. But if I do 'em for myself, I'm not allowed to sell 'em—or even give 'em away."

F I R S T   D E E R

For the initial day or so, the carcass hung from a tree in front of the house. Then it disappeared—moved into a crowded, rickety barn.

"I just hung it up there [on the tree] to show my friends," the hunter says with a grin. He has been hunting since he was a small boy, but this is his first deer.

Eviscerated and hung so it will bleed dry, the deer is a macabre, even disturbing sight, especially next to the ruddy-cheeked hunter who stares expressionless into the camera lens while posing with his trophy.

But the deer is more than a prize. It will also provide many meals for the hunter's family during the approaching winter. And one can be sure that, come next season, the hunter will be in the woods once more, looking for number two.

T O O L   T A L E S

The Tool Barn in Hull's Cove, near Bar Harbor, is open "by chance or appointment" year round, though one usually can find the place available for some serious browsing every day in the summer and early fall.

This is not a tool boutique of shiny new equipment, stiff leather work belts, and aprons festooned with manufacturers' logos. Almost everything here has the beautiful dull patina of hard use—of tools that could tell tales of barns raised, floors laid, and walls built.

Skip Brack runs the business with a practiced, diffident air, and if you can't find what you want, he can probably get it for you. Some tools bought here are doubtless put back to work—by craftsmen looking for just the right implement. Many, however, are bought less as woodworking tools and more as pieces of sculpture, ornaments from an age when people worked with their hands and backs to create things of beauty and utility.

F O R G I N G   T R A D I T I O N

Save for the occasional boom box or the fluorescent lighting or the giveaway slogan on a baseball hat, this picture could have been made in the last century. In this factory, much of the technology—not to mention the machinery itself—is that old.

Sitting on the Bangor side of the Penobscot River, the Snow & Nealley plant has been making garden and logging tools since 1864. Today, the company enjoys a reputation for excellence and durability that no amount of high-priced hype can duplicate. The men who work here (there are few women) are accustomed to heat, noise, and molten metal, namely the high-carbon steel from which they fashion everything from garden trowel to ax to lumberman's peavey.

A modern drop forge would almost certainly not look like the one pictured here. It dwarfs its operator, who is about to place a molten bar inside the machine, step on the hydraulic release, and—in one huge slam—create a maul or hatchet or ax.

Some two stories high, Snow & Nealley's ancient drop forge is a throwback to the time when, lacking sophisticated equipment to measure tolerances and metal fatigue, designers and inventors produced the heavy, over-engineered machinery so typical of the Industrial Revolution.

Big-shouldered, raw-boned behemoths, these are machines that were meant to last—like the tools they produce.

WINTER'S TALE

Maine winters were not made for cathedral ceilings. Houses here were built to contain heat, not dissipate it skyward, so there is always a certain coziness in the many older, lower-ceilinged houses down east. That's why, too, the rooms tend to be small and numerous, rather than large and few.

In the deep cold of a Maine winter, when the temperature hovers in the teens, the wind is moaning, and a full moon spreads brilliant light over ice-covered roads, it is good to be indoors, warmed by the woodstove.

It is even better, if you are six years old, to be in your mother's lap listening to a story.

L O A D E D   F O R   B E A R

The joke among the field biologists of Maine's Department of Inland Fisheries and Wildlife is that when tracking bears in the snowbound woods, you go until your truck gets stuck, switch to snowmobiles until they get stuck, then switch to snowshoes until *you* get stuck.

The annual field survey is vital to estimating Maine's black bear population. Directed every winter from the department's office in Bangor, it enables biologists to extrapolate the bear population throughout the state and also helps determine the number of animals that can be taken during the fall hunting season.

The survey is conducted with scientific precision, ranging far afield in the Maine woods, into areas specially selected as having a representative sample of the state's bear population. It's a far cry from the necessarily haphazard field studies of previous decades. Back then, black bear surveyors—working without the benefit of four-wheel drive trucks or snowmobiles—traveled only as far as their snowshoes could carry them.

Randy Cross, one of the modern biologists, is a strapping, loquacious thirty-seven year old whose love of the great Maine outdoors led him to field work some fourteen years ago. It's a measure of the kind of people who do this work that Randy ate virtually no store-bought meat through much of his childhood. All that his family needed, they either cultivated, shot, or caught.

On this day, Randy's team (one of two working in the area) includes Lindsay Tudor, a biologist and mother of two whose expertise includes not only bears but birds, and Duggins (Doogie) Wroe, a field technician who has tracked and surveyed wildlife both in Maine and in the American West.

The initial foray into the woods, on a cold, overcast March day in snowbound Ashland, Maine, proves arduous and frustrating. Randy and his team are guided by a handheld receiver that picks up signals from the battery-powered transmitter on each tagged bear's neck collar. Deciding on one promising area, the biologists trudge with snowshoes and backpacks more than a mile into the woods, following an ominously uniform signal. Each bear's transmitter is sensitive to motion and will vary its signal whenever a hibernating bear moves in its sleep. An unchanging signal like this one usually means a dead bear. When they finally reach their destination and Randy begins digging to find the den, the team uncovers news that's simultaneously good and bad.

There, a few yards down, is not a hibernating bear and her cubs, or even a dead bear, but a broken collar that probably got caught in a branch or tree limb and torn. The team's trip, spanning long, difficult hours, has been futile.

"Let's find . . . some bear cubs," Randy says, frustration in his voice. The light is failing and the weather is turning nasty. There will be only one more chance to find bears this day, and Randy, Lindsay, and Doogie hope that luck will be with them.

It is. Selecting another spot a few miles away, they find a hibernating mother bear and three newborns curled up in a

huge, rotted-out cedar trunk, not even a half-mile from the road. As they near the site, drawn both by the beeping of the sow's tracking collar and the audible cries of her three cubs, the team feels a near-freezing drizzle begin to fall.

Randy's first goal is to anesthetize the mother bear, lying in partial hibernation in the century-old trunk, her wide-awake young huddled beside her. He readies a spring-loaded dart stick and gingerly pokes the sow in the rump. The bear lets out a startled growl but fortunately doesn't come roaring out of the tree trunk. (How dangerous are black bears? Though they aren't normally aggressive, their jaws are like vises, and their long claws are knife-sharp. It's not for mere show that each of the survey-team leaders carries a loaded .357 magnum on his hip.)

"We'll wait ten minutes and see how she's doing," Randy says. Because he could only reach the bear's fat-laden hindquarters, there is a chance the anesthetic will dissipate into her tissue, not her bloodstream. To be on the safe side, Randy gives her a second shot, and that does the trick.

With the sow out cold, Randy and his colleagues reach into the tree trunk and bring out the squealing cubs, followed by the mother, who is laid on her side on a yellow plastic tarp. As a necessary precaution, the sow's legs are tied together by thick nylon rope before any examinations begin.

Barely a foot long and not at all happy, the cubs clamber frantically over the team members, but they quickly calm down when they are held closely and protectively. The team weighs and measures each bear, logging the information; they then tag the cubs' ears with numbered plastic markers. Finally, the mother—still sleeping peacefully on the ground—is given a teeth-to-tail examination. Randy gently strokes the unconscious sow as Lindsay, kneeling above, cradles its huge head in her hands—a Pietà in the Maine woods.

With all data collected, mother and offspring are carefully placed back in their den, but not before each cub is rubbed with a viscous mixture of cedar oil, to mask any human scent they may have picked up during the exam. The sun is beginning to set. It's time to go home.

After a thirteen-hour day, Randy, Lindsay, and Doogie rendezvous with the other survey team on a frozen logging trail, heft the snowmobiles back onto the trucks, and head back into Ashland and the motel. Everyone eats a hearty dinner before turning in at nine-thirty.

Dawn will come soon enough, and the entire operation will be repeated until, at last, the survey is done.

WELDER

In a state where secondary roads, not highways, predominate, trains are still critical for moving freight. As a result, the demand for maintenance and repair of railcars provides much-needed jobs for skilled workers like this welder, who is employed by the Bangor & Aroostook Railroad.

T H E   W H A L E

It lies huge and dead on the town beach—a fifty-eight-foot, forty-five-ton male finback whale that drowned at sea after becoming entangled in fishing lines. The incoming tide has carried the magnificent carcass and laid it gently on the shore, bringing to Lubec another problem that the town doesn't need.

For the first day or so the whale, lying on its side with its eyes closed, its mouth agape, is literally the biggest thing in town. Townsfolk and tourists flock to it, marveling at its size. At high tide, when the whale is half covered by water, it bobs languidly up and down in the icy-cold summertime sea as children in shorts heave rocks at its carcass. At low tide, when the whale is fully beached, one can walk its length on both sides, touch its bloated body (which feels like an inflated rubber raft), and run a hand along its mouth, feeling the bristle-like strands of the baleen plates that once strained the nutrients the whale sucked from the sea.

Of course, this isn't the first time the Bay of Fundy has surrendered its dead—simultaneously, the body of a five-hundred-pound gray seal washed up on shore only a few miles away. And longtime Lubecker David Rier recalls the dead whale that washed up on Campobello years ago, and he remembers the vexing time the authorities had in getting rid of it. ("They towed it out, but the tide brought it right back.")

Surveying the whale in a chill morning fog, Lubec diver Butch Huntley notes that the finback is the second largest creature in the world, (after the blue whale) and can grow to

more than eighty feet in length. Though somewhat smaller than that, Lubec's whale is plenty big enough for Mark Decoteau, the town manager. He has been on the job barely a year, and he is now finding that disposing of it is shaping up to be the town's, and therefore his, exclusive responsibility.

"If this whale were still alive [the state and federal governments] would spend $4 million to try to save it," says Decoteau as he views the ripening remains along with about a dozen or so onlookers. "But now that it's dead, there isn't a federal or state agency that has a dollar to help us."

Not that he didn't ask. In the first forty-eight hours after the whale's appearance on the beach, the wiry, bespectacled Decoteau, a former career army officer, rode the

phone. He spoke with, among others, the Maine Department of Marine Resources, the National Marine Fisheries Service, the U.S. Coast Guard, the College of the Atlantic, and the New England Aquarium, seeking assistance.

"On Sunday," he says, "the people from the aquarium showed up, took samples, and said they weren't interested in doing anything further. Monday morning, I was told by our harbormaster that the Coast Guard and Marine Resources were going to tow it back out to sea." Instead, however, the Coast Guard washed its hands of the beast, arguing that since the whale was no longer a threat to navigation, it was not a Coast Guard responsibility. Marine Resources said it had no vessels big enough to do the towing.

"It's a rare occurrence for a whale to wash up on a beach with so many people around," notes marine biologist Anne McGhie of Pembroke. But, she adds that at any given time, "there are at least two or three dead whales that nobody sees floating in the waters off the East Coast." Many of them are victims of collisions with ships in the north Atlantic, though a comparative few will have run afoul of the fishing gear of lobstermen and gillnetters.

Still, McGhie notes, most lobstermen work inshore with comparatively short lines that have little, if any, impact on the great mammals. It's the longer lines, or the poorly laid lines, much farther out to sea that can pose a threat not just to whales but to boats as well. "I remember being offshore and seeing two hundred feet of line floating on the surface," McGhie says. That kind of thing can foul a propeller or encumber a sea creature, often with disastrous results for both.

The problem is exacerbated by environmental radicals who want to "save" the whales by banning all commercial fishing in New England, even in the absence of any convincing proof that fishing poses a significant threat to whales in these waters. Like people, whales die. It's just that their presence in death is harder to ignore.

Once, years ago, a much smaller minke whale washed up on the beach at Cape Elizabeth, near Portland. Decoteau recalls that disposal of that carcass, less than a third the size of the finback, cost the town upwards of $9,000—a sum that Lubec, one of the poorest towns in Maine, simply doesn't have.

"First I was told to take it to our landfill—which, of course the DEP [Maine Department of Environmental Protection] closed four months ago," laments Decoteau. "Then I was told to bury it on the beach. I was told to bury it on land. I was told to cut it up and take it to our transfer station . . . which doesn't take pathological waste."

Butch Huntley, who has joined Decoteau on the now chill, fog-shrouded beach, offers his own tongue-in-cheek solution. "I suggested what they do is tow it over to Campobello and beach it there," he says with a sly grin.

Finally it becomes clear that, whatever course Decoteau decides to take, it is going to be on his head—and be paid for out of Lubec's meager budget.

That's fitting in a way. Lubeckers, like many of their down east neighbors, have grown accustomed to solving their own problems with little or no outside help. Decoteau,

a West Point graduate who grew up in Maine, says he gravitated down east because the region has retained many qualities of life that were disappearing in the more developed parts of the state, qualities like independence and self-reliance. The people here are "harder," he says. "They play rougher and just have a different outlook on life. They're much more independent, too. A lot of that has to do with the fact that, when you're out on a boat and it's just you and the Atlantic, you kind of have to make do."

That resourcefulness shows up in times of trouble, says Decoteau. "If it's just a normal, routine kind of thing, they don't go out of their way. But if somebody's in real trouble—if it's life-threatening in any way—the whole community will be there." Many here, he goes on, view the state government and, by extension, the federal government as nettlesome intrusions—or, at least, no help at all. After all, Lubeckers would argue, the feds closed down McCurdy's Smokehouse for no good reason. Just recently, state money was cut for local fire fighting, meaning that towns like Lubec, whose land is 80 percent forested, have to depend strictly on unpaid volunteers if the worst happens.

Even the outfits that wanted to preserve the region's beauty did so at an awful price—buying up parcels of land to keep it virgin, then balking at paying their fair share of taxes. All these things weigh on Mark Decoteau's mind when he decides that his only course is to bury the whale where it lies.

"I've got liability here that I don't want to think about,"

Decoteau says in the early morning fog as Billy Ramsdell's backhoe begins an artful minuet of digging in the beach's solid clay. "I'm probably violating fifty-three state regulations here," says Decoteau, "but we really don't have any choice."

Back and forth Ramsdell maneuvers his machine, scooping up great gobs of clay that a front-end loader then pushes to one side, creating a small mountain near the whale's giant body. Larger and larger the grave becomes until finally there is a gaping hole sixty-five feet long and fifteen feet deep. The plan is to dig the hole as close to the whale as possible, whereupon the backhoe and loader would nudge the stinking carcass into it.

All goes according to schedule until the very end. As Ramsdell is making the final gouges in the earth, near the whale's head, the clay under the creature's great middle begins to give way. Then, in silent slow motion, the huge carcass rolls over and into the hole. All that remains visible now is the finback's massive head, and Ramsdell gently sculpts away the remaining bits of clay to allow the beast its final rest.

By mid-afternoon the beach is back to normal.

When the final costs are tallied, the town of Lubec has to pay only $260, for Ramsdell's time and that of the other men who helped with the burial. It is money the town can scant afford, but it is no $9,000.

And Lubeckers have done it their way, without help.

As they always will.

JUDITH GOODMAN

TECHNICAL NOTES

All photographs in this project were made in black and white with Hasselblad and Mamiya medium-format cameras.

Earlier photographs were made on Ilford XP-2 film, later images on Kodak T400CN. Film processing was done by StarLab Photographic Services of Bethesda, Maryland.

Lighting ranged from available light to multiple strobe setups designed to approximate or augment existing light.

All images were printed by the photographer using a Beseler 4x5 enlarger and Zone VI Cold Light head. Prints were made on Agfa Portriga Rapid, grades 2 and 3, or on Agfa Multicontrast Classic.

The author gratefully acknowledges a generous materials grant from Agfa for the making of production and exhibition prints.

Above my desk in Washington is a yellowed cartoon from *The New Yorker*. "Well, it's good," says the publisher to the bearded author sitting before him, "but people just don't write books all by themselves anymore."

Well, yes and no.

I write the books I photograph; I photograph the books I write. Still, many other people helped bring this project to life.

Thanks first and always to my wife and partner, Judy, whose critical eye and ear I cherish almost as much as her love and her laughter.

Thanks, too, to my agent Paul Mahon, who helped start the rollercoaster ride to publication.

In Washington, Pat Marshall Whitehead of Pat Marshall Design once again took all the pieces and created a beautiful package for them.

At Down East Books, I was made to feel welcome from the start by Tom Fernald, my publisher. Chris Cornell, my editor, wielded his pencil with deftness and restraint, for which I will always be grateful.

Finally, Fred and Nancy Hastings of the *Downeast Coastal Press* provided Judy and me not only with friendship through the years but also with a valuable sounding board for my story and picture ideas.

The talent and caring of all these people helped give form to this book.

My thanks to them all.

—FVR

ACKNOWLEDGMENTS